THE CATS:

VOLUME 1

ON THE BANDSTAND OF LIFE
WITH MASTER MUSICIANS

BY JAKE FEINBERG

Edited by David Lasocki

PORTLAND, OREGON
INSTANT HARMONY
2019

Copyright © Jake Feinberg, 2019

Published by Instant Harmony, a creation of DavidLasocki.com
www.davidlasocki.com

Cover design by Laura Serrano-Silva

ISBN 9781702112451

TABLE OF CONTENTS

Foreword by George Marsh — vii
Introduction by Jake Feinberg — ix

Part 1. In the Studio — 1
Steve Gadd — 5
Dennis Coffey — 10
Jim Keltner — 16
Joe Sample — 22
Danny Kortchmar — 27
Leland Sklar — 35
Randy Brecker — 41
Ron Tutt — **47**
Buzz Feiten — **51**
Chuck Rainey — 57
Leon "Ndugu" Chandler — 61
Emil Richards — 67
David Spinozza — 76

Part 2. In Memoriam Neal Casal — 81

Part 3. Wizards — 101
Larry Coryell — 105
Lenny White — 111
Dave Liebman — 118
Kenny Burrell — **123**
Greg Errico — 128
Steve Swallow — 134
Billy Cobham — 145
David Lindley — 153
David Garibaldi — 162
Pat Martino — 172

Index of Names — 183

" ... it is very easy to get lost in the wilderness of imaginations and lose the perspective of life.... By exploring deep within ourselves, by the method of transcendental, deep meditation, we arrive to fathom the ocean of life energy present within ourselves, and tap the power of cosmic intelligence, and bring the force of eternity and cosmic energy in the present, right here and now, and be what we want to be, what we ought to be, and what we deserve to be."

Maharishi Mahesh Yogi, "The Untapped Source of Power that Lies within" (talk, 1967)

FOREWORD

BY GEORGE MARSH

Jake Feinberg is a treasure! When he called and asked me if I would like to be interviewed, I immediately sensed something different was going on here. Jake wanted to know what I *really* thought about what it's like to be an elder musician and how my history as a player and recording artist was somehow different from what's going on in so much of today's pop music.

After our first interview, I realized that he had brought out something that other interviewers never seemed to get to—the bliss, love, driving force, spirituality, importance, seriousness, individuality, and joy of being a creative musician. He wanted to know *why* we love music so much and *what* we know about it that tends not to be honored in the media today. I found myself speaking to someone who truly wanted to know what makes me tick. The trust was palpable, and we were immediately old friends.

Jake has a magical ability to get us musicians talking. About what we feel about our experiences, on and off stage. What it's like to live the life of a musician, both now and in the past. After listening to his many interviews over the years, I am struck by how similar we musicians all are and yet how each of us has a unique approach to getting to that place of deep communication.

Jake knows that music is about trust and love between fellow musicians and sharing that with the people. To be interviewed by him is a lot like improvising with my fellow musician friends. It's as if Jake is the rhythm section for a series of freely improvised solos. Each interview (solo) is different, guided by Jake's deep listening skills and honesty. His enthusiasm is contagious.

We're fortunate to have Jake doing this important work!

George Marsh has taught drum set and rhythm theory at Sonoma State University, California and the University of California at Santa Cruz since 1982. He has had a distinguished career as a percussionist and drummer in classical, jazz, and popular settings, and has also composed percussion music for movies and classical concerts. Among the musicians he has played and recorded with are Mose Allison, David Grisman, Joe Henderson, Terry Riley, Barbra Streisand, and Denny Zeitlin. He is also the author of the landmark book *Inner Drumming* (Sher Music, 2016).

INTRODUCTION

BY JAKE FEINBERG

The Cats! Volume 1 is a book that explores the 4Ls: lessons in leadership, love, life, and lineage as told by musical masters.

These stories come from radio interviews conducted on The Jake Feinberg Show, an extra-terrestrial radio program designed to connect humanity and inspire people to be themselves, through long-form interviews with artists who were creating long before I, the host, was born (1978). I have been using my platform to highlight luminaries of the music and entertainment world as well as the accompanists who served the music and helped cultivate the songs that led some individuals to become stars.

Since January 2011, I have conducted over 1,000 radio interviews with artists who cross over all musical genres. I get to explore the regionalism of music in this country before full inter-connection. What that means is that cats were able to come together in an organic fashion, be discovered, and wind up becoming units on the bandstand for many, many years. What happened then is that the vocabulary of music was expanded and extended.

One of the things that's been refreshing on this journey after doing so many interviews with The Cats is that initially you believe musicians are always searching for that state of bliss, when in actuality they are doing it to f***ing live.

It has been my responsibility as a journalist to bridge the gap of full interconnection. The extra-terrestrial telephonic hangs on PowerTalk 1210 continue as I forge into the regional rhythm sections of Chicago, New Orleans and Atlanta. Cats like Paul Boudreaux, Big Chief Monk Boudreaux and Rodney Justo, Ron Steele, Bill Stewart, and Rick Hinkle. The Left Coast was not neglected, as I tracked down the mercurial John Morell and Ray Neapolitan, Fred Tackett, Don Menza, the late David Axelrod, and the late Wilton Felder: studio sharks whose job it was to create the vibe and swing on TV shows, cartoons, and seminal albums that stand the test of time.

Thanks to Kevin Calabro (Royal Potato Family), I got hip to a bevy of younger burgeoning artists who play music as if their life depended on it. Cats like Ethan Miller, Matthew Waterfall Gibbs, Sam Blasucci, Neal Casal, Brian Haas, Jeff Hill, and Frank LoCrasto, who are part of the cyclical nature of musical lineage.

Music is the language of the soul. Rhythm is love. And that is what my show is about. *The Cats!* Volume 1 focuses on group dynamics, how to overcome adversity, the individual rhythm of each player, and how that has impacted the lineage of all the types of music and the musicians that play them.

As much as I love the music, I love the musicians more. My show is about expressing individual taste, it's not about uniformity. We have enough of that going on in our society and it's hurting us.

The urban legend of Detroit is only for those generations who were not alive during the time when that city epitomized "Asphalt Canyon Blues."

In the 21st century, the so-called digital age, the roles of a producer and a musician have devolved into a potpourri of inanimate objects: the number of records you sell, how to make a hit, the drum machine, and a shrinking, more rigid music industry. Yet in the past, enclaves of regional music crossed the great divide from Arkansas to Toronto. Leadership was defined as getting out of the way and letting the wolf howl, or letting the music play the band.

I'm into the esoteric part of music, and the big ears. I'm definitely into enlarging hearts the way Tisziji Muñoz does. He gave me my spirit name, Sem Lodro (Spirit of Mind). This coincides with "The Dao," which has filled me with a resilience and an urgency to pursue the truth, or the closest thing to it. Receiving the Dao felt as if old chapters of my life closed and a new one began. As a Daoist, my duty through my work is to help sentient beings transcend the cycle of birth and death. Cultivating the Dao lies in practice and not in empty talk. The Dao begins with self-expectation (introspection) and not placing demands on others, but rather, inspiring them to find their true nature. Wishing only to find my Buddha nature, I dedicate this book to the goddess Laomu. Thanks to Kim Yong for being my guarantor!

This whole broadcasting experience has been aided and abetted by a tribe of not-so-usual suspects. Artists who I had never personally met but who "go there" with me in a live, long-form, improvisational, free-form radio setting. They have helped me see the big picture, enjoying the forbidden fruit along the way. My knowledge comes from real peeps and from experience.

Cats like Ahmad Jamal, John McLaughlin, George Porter, Jr., Huey Lewis, Steve Cropper, George Marsh, Tony Leone, Max Weinberg, Johnny Mathis, Billy Harper, Steve Earle, Rita Coolidge, Airto Moreira, Justine Bennett, Butch Trucks, David Murray, Bob Weir, Merle Haggard, Martha Reeves, Ken Babbs, Wavy Gravy, Oteil Burbridge, and Sunshine Kesey.

Over the last two years I've taken The Jake Feinberg Show on the road. The greatest development was the subtle but significant transition from telephonic hangs with the cats to meeting them and conducting interviews in person. The actual human connection (still using technology) is vital for societal transformation and enlightenment. Some of the stories you are about to indulge in came from interviews conducted in person on the new media, driving consciousness in an instantaneous improvisational format that can inspire regular peeps.

Mark Zuckerberg was instrumental in helping The Jake Feinberg Show grow its reach worldwide with the advent of the Facebook Live feature. Going live started with Tower of Power in January 2017. JFS has done several hundred Facebook Live interviews with cats like Jerry Cortez and Rocco Prestia, David Garibaldi and Doc Kupka. Then it was on to Pat Martino and Carmen Intorre, Bob Mann, Allan Schwartzberg, Karina Rykman, Merry Pranksters Ken Babbs and George Walker, Dom Famularo, David Margen, Dean Brown, Alex Ligertwood, Tony Braunagel, Skip Rickert, Farmer Dave Scher, Tisziji Muñoz, Dr. Patrick Gleeson, and James Gadson.

Multiple trips to Northern and Southern California, including forays into Napa Valley to chronicle the correlation of heart, health, and wine. Being able to interview the likes of Michael Mondavi, Robert Biale, Anthony Truchard, Dorothy Rossi, Dr. Jerry Sepps, Jay Heminway, and Dario Sattui—Renaissance men and women who can testify to the sacred mantras of original family wine makers. Thank you to Dr. Tedd Goldfinger for hipping me to some hip cats.

Back to the musicians, I found myself in New York, Nashville, Atlanta, New Orleans (three times), Colorado, Santa Fe, Portland Oregon, and California once more doing Facebook Live interviews. The video component of the JFS has expanded my reach internationally because of opportunities to interview musicians from India (Shahid Parvez Khan), Africa (Sikiru Adepoju), and Jamaica (Carlton "Santa" Davis). Consider the JFS a three-headed content monster, disseminating information in audio, video, and print formats. Thousands of radio interviews, hundreds of Facebook Live interviews, and transcriptions from these transmissions that have pinged and ponged across the digital globe, inspiring people to be themselves over the past three years.

I have also devoted my program to the Divine Feminine Spirit—strong, emboldened women such as Dayna Seraye, who told me in our first interview: "Calling myself a priestess very much has a feeling to it. There's a feeling of devotion, of being devoted to the Divine. For me it is often in the form of the divine mother. Being in devotion and living my life purposefully in devotion. For me healing, wholeness, balance, beauty can be the norm on our planet. It's very simple really: it's living a devotional life where I can be of service.

"When we stay on the level of the mind and the concept, it doesn't go very far in. When we drop down to the level of the heart, all of a sudden we have a greater capacity to understand something on a different level. When it goes down to the level of the soul, we just simply live it.

"I agree that this empowerment of women is gaining momentum. It's pretty accepted in the circles I run in that this is happening. It's a reclaiming of the feminine, of the ways of the feminine: in both men and women is what we really need, not just being female. It's an intuition, it's a softening, it's a way of allowing, it's a receptivity. It's about connecting to the earth, feeling relationships and not being so rigid that we're stuck in our own process. Actually being in a fluid relationship and dancing with all of life."

I've interviewed women such as Dayna who have experienced the roller coasters of life, and come around stronger, more dedicated to their craft, family, and higher purpose.

The great drummer Pete Lind told me:

"If you play music, you live a long time, because you're always learning. You never stop learning, because there's no end to it. The Jake Feinberg Show is going to go on forever, because you're interested in something that has no end."

Even if my sacred journey does go on forever, the time has come to put together a book of radio interviews that speak to enlightenment, expanding consciousness, and inspiration.

This book and the radio interviews would not be possible without the support and loyalty of my sponsors: Abbott Taylor (Abbott Taylor Jewelers), Butch "Horn Man" Diggs (Diggs Dental), Craig Pretzinger (Pretzinger Allstate Insurance), Todd Rockoff (Tucson Jewish Community Center), the late Jay Heminway (Green and Red Vineyard), and Dr. Tedd Goldfinger (Renaud Society). My deepest respect for these individuals, all the people who have the privilege to work for them, and their belief in yours truly.

Also, I want to shout a big thanks to Jim Parisi, our fearless leader at Powertalk 1210 (an Internet Broadcasting Station). And a big shout out to my great kids, Hannah and Aja. Their love and support continue to inspire and push me to further myself and my show. They inspire me in their world view and outlook on all areas of life. They have ridden the road untraveled with me and incurred the high highs and low lows of doing something completely entrepreneurial and unique.

Finally, I am forever indebted to my tireless and accessible editor and publisher, David Lasocki, for his essential work in getting this book across the proverbial finish line. Among other things, he taught me in a practical way how "content dictates form," in this case leaving behind the played-out question-and-answer format for interviews and moving into a more free-flowing style with vignettes as statements of life. David reminds us by his example how to lead with the heart. I wish all burgeoning authors could work with him and his company, Instant Harmony.

The Jake Feinberg Show:
Powertalk 1210; http://powertalk.live/
www.jakefeinbergshow.com

PART 1

IN THE STUDIO

The studio cats represented by these interviews played on thousands of sessions and hundreds of gold records. They cut their teeth on the bandstand with the luminaries who came before them and gained experience in all forms of music: no holds barred.

The studios stretched from Los Angeles and San Francisco to Chicago and Detroit, from Macon, Nashville, and Memphis to New York. Everybody was in the same room, plugged into a direct box with minimal mic placement. These were spaces where jingles, commercials, and cartoons were cut, and hit records were galvanized—by largely unsung musicians.

Let us help to sing their song now.

STEVE GADD

Steve Gadd is one of the world's foremost drummers. He came out of the U.S. Army Band in the early 1960s and wound up in Rochester, NY sitting in with Jack McDuff and Shirley Scott. He also began a lifelong collaboration with Chuck and Gap Mangione.

Upon arriving in New York, Steve made a name for himself in the studios playing with Paul Simon, Chet Baker, Bob James, Chick Corea, and Steely Dan. Steve never overplays and always gives the song what it needs.

Among the excerpts included here are: how Steve almost lost everything to addiction and how he overcame it, the studio scene in New York when he arrived, waking up every day and being open to not knowing, and how the death of Eric Clapton's son affected him.

Light and Dark

I ended up going into rehab and I had to move out of New York. I had been playing under the influence for so long I wasn't sure what was going to happen. When I finally did go back and play music, I have good friends in the business. And being able to go back to music straight and still love playing and being in the same situation with people and not use anymore—it was great to have that.

I could have lost it all and I didn't. Looking back on it, being able to come back to music helped save my life. I don't think drugs make you play better, but they can ease whatever pain you're going through to help you concentrate on something that makes you feel good.

A lot of times people turn to drugs because there's a loss someplace else, or there's a part of their life that's fallen apart. You lose a loved one or you split up and you have little kids involved and you can't see them.

Aside from just taking drugs to stay awake so you could take the work, there's something else they do. They numb some pain and allow you to at least focus on something that's making you feel good. Those years it was the music for me.

I'm very happy I'm alive. I've got a great wife, Carol. I've got four beautiful kids, three grandkids, five dogs. You can't just take things for granted. You've got to work at being grateful. In all situations there's two ways to look at things. You've got to try to look on the bright side, look up at the light and try to go that way. Be grateful and try to remember what you have to be thankful for, and try to be forgiving of whatever resentments and angers you have, Because if you give in to anger, resentment, and revenge you throw your life away.

There's a lot of things I did under the influence of drugs that I don't remember, 'cause I was on automatic pilot. I ended up in rehab and in a twelve-step program. That's when I really started to learn about spirituality and a higher power, gratitude. They're just things I didn't know about. They don't teach you that stuff in school. Those are real important lessons. To be able to say you're sorry, to wake up in the morning and give thanks for having a shot at another day. At the end of the day, to say thank you for all the opportunities that you had.

Those are things I learned in a program. They have programs for all types of situations for people who think they are terminally unique. We're not alone, we're all in this thing together.

Let's say I'm playing a live show in front of a sold-out arena and the people are really excited to see whoever I'm working for. I go up there and if something's not right in the monitor, I spend the whole night fussing and thinking about what I don't have, rather than looking around and being thankful for what I do have. If you can't appreciate the energy you get back from the audience, you can throw that right out the window.

Then I'm Open

The best way is to lead by example. It's nothing that has to be loud. People are always looking, even when you don't know they're looking. You don't have to be a band leader to live like someone who wants to make a difference.

The best days of my life are the days that I wake up and I don't know, and then I'm open. You can't always give someone the answer, if they're not asking the question. You have to time when you think it's the right time to give information. If it's not the right time, it's not the right information.

I'm not in a situation where I'm the leader a lot, but that's how I deal with things. How I act and how I react. I think you have to react that you are a leader.

People who were recording for a living made it a point to get in to play. A lot of times you'd get the call if the first call wasn't available. You'd never go in starting at the top of the list. You'd always try to go to New York to get on the list by doing something that sounded good, by playing in a rehearsal band, by meeting musicians and exchanging numbers. Music is a word-of-mouth business.

An Old Hearse

I used to participate in jam sessions in my hometown of Rochester, NY. They had Sunday matinees where they brought in organ groups. It would be 4–6 pm and then at another club would do 5–7 pm and then another club that would be 6–8 pm. Everybody who was in the first club would end up in the last club. There would be a line of drummers waiting to play, a line of horn players. Those were those days. That's when a lot of guys who weren't working playing music for a living got to sit in and develop their thing.

I got to sit in with Jack McDuff, Hank Marr, Gene Ludwig, Groove Holmes, and Shirley Scott—anyone who was coming through town. They'd do a week in Rochester and then go to Buffalo, Syracuse, Albany, wherever the clubs were. They called it the Chitlin Circuit because everybody in the band would have their gear packed into a van or an old hearse. A lot of times these bands would buy an old hearse for their weekly run of shows. I don't know where all these clubs were, but these guys kept working. They'd finish the circuit and come back around again.

End up Being Your Voice

When I first came to New York I took anything I could get. Rehearsals, demos; most of it didn't pay. It was a matter of playing with as many different people as you could and trying to get your name out there.

If you let the music be the inspiration and you find the right thing for the music, chances are it will end up being your voice without you trying to make it anything other than what's right for the music.

That Is My Attitude

I had respect that I had a chance to play with Ron Carter and Roland Hanna in *Concierto* by the Jim Hall sextet. Back in the mid-70s when I got called to play a date with people I had listened to as a kid, who were my heroes, making a living recording great music, that was a tremendous opportunity. I went in with great admiration and desire to make it and do the best I could. To pay homage to those guys and be respectful to them and play as well as I could.

That is my attitude when I go to work, in terms of the music and the people who call you. You want to give them your best shot. You want to be really present and there for them. Back in those days when I was called to play with Ron Carter and Roland Hanna, it made me be on my best behavior.

These are the guys you dream of playing with. Richard Tee and Cornell Dupree, Bernard Purdie, Chuck Rainey: to me they were superstars. Because of how they played and who they'd played with. They played with people who wrote the book on certain kinds of music. They defined the grooves in a lot of areas of playing.

When you're a young musician trying to get established in this business, those are the people you want to play with you, so they can recommend you and you can play with them some more. You don't want it to be your last time. That's the kind of energy and self-discipline you put into those things.

I'm A Father

When Eric Clapton's son died, I couldn't believe it. It devastated me trying to understand how anyone could overcome that kind of pain.

I had worked with Russ Titelman a lot over the years. He had produced some of Eric's music. I ran into him and asked him how Eric was doing. I didn't know Eric personally, but I'm a father: I could identify with that kind of devastation.

I said, "Man, if there's anything I could ever do, let me know." Eric was in a situation where he was looking to make a change, and Russ recommended me. I don't know if Russ did it from a musical point of view, or from the point of view of our conversation, but it was after that that I got a call to join Eric. I was very excited to do that.

To be in a situation and work with people who, just by their reputation and what they've accomplished musically, you put their name on the marquee and the show sells out in a matter of minutes. It's pretty amazing to be part of that.

The people are coming to see Eric or coming to see James Taylor or coming to see Paul Simon. To be a part of that energy and to be able to feel that you contributed to making it as good for the people as it could be, that's a nice thing to be a part of.

DENNIS COFFEY

Guitarist Dennis Coffey comes from Detroit, Michigan, one of the regions of this country that had its own sound. He came up during the birth of rock and roll, and because of that, he was not restricted to any guidelines, rule, or literature. In other words, he could make up his own rules and develop his own original sound while cutting records. He joined Motown and became a Funk Brother with James Jamerson, Jack Ashford, Eddie "Bongo" Brown, Earl Van Dyke, Johnny Griffith, Uriel Jones, Richard "Pistol" Allen, Joe Messina, Eddie Willis, Robert White, and Jack Brokensha.

Coffey's guitar can be heard on iconic records by The Temptations, Edwin Starr, Wilson Pickett, Diana Ross, and George Clinton. He has been a prolific leader and producer in the studio for years, working hand and glove with his partner, Mike Theodore, at Sussex Records, Westbound, and MoWest. The two of them discovered the folk-rock singer Sixto Rodriguez in Detroit. The albums they produced for him lay dormant for years, until the iconic documentary *Searching for Sugar Man* was released in 2012.

I did two radio interviews with Dennis: January and July 2019. We talked about how his development coincided with the birth of rock music, the magic ear of Quincy Jones, the recording techniques of The Funk Brothers in the studio, and being recruited by Jerry Wexler.

He's Facing the Wall

Sixto Rodriguez, Sugar Man, had a single deal with Harry Balk. He did like four singles, and then Harry dropped him from Impact Records. Rodriguez's manager called me and said, "He doesn't have a deal. Why don't you go hear him play?"

Rodriguez was playing at a place called The Sewer, which was along the Detroit River. Mike Theodore and I go into this place, and it's all foggy, and river freighters are going by on the Detroit River, and here is this guy singing but he's facing the wall. That was Rodriguez. The guy was so shy, when we first got him in the studio, we had to bring him in by himself. We recorded him and his guitar for the first four songs and built a band around him.

People in the US did not respond to Rodriguez when his first albums *Cold Fact* and *Coming from Reality* came out. So Clarence Avant dropped him from the label, Sussex Records. They did sell in Australia and South Africa. Everyone thought Rodriguez was dead. Mike Theodore saw that on the Internet and told the people that Rodriguez was alive and well and living in Detroit. The rest is history, resulting in the award-winning documentary *Searching for Sugar Man*, which made Rodriguez an international star.

I Have No Idea

My mom said I could name every song on the radio when I was 2. I did my first record date and took my first two guitar solos—and got paid for it—at the age of 15. At 16, in the metropolitan Detroit area, you had teen clubs every Friday night, and if you were a good band you could do weddings and things on Saturday.

Rock and roll was just starting and it was being created as we were learning it. So the only way you could learn that stuff was by listening and copying what guys were doing on record. You'd ask a guitar teacher, "What's Chuck Berry doing?" The guy would say, "I have no idea." You had to learn it by listening to the records. There were about twenty bands doing that. So by the time we were old enough to work at the bars, we were already equipped with a huge repertoire, 'cause we knew all the songs.

Big-Boy Leagues Right There

I played with The Funk Brothers on a daily basis. We'd arrive for a session, which was three hours. We'd get there at 10 or 11 o'clock in the morning, and usually the only people in the studio would be the eleven funk brothers, the arranger, and the producer.

They'd put a master rhythm chart in front of us, and the first job of the day was to read the chart as written. Then if the arranger was happy with how you were interpreting the written music, and the producer wanted a little extra, you could suggest some licks.

Our job was to record one song every hour with no mistakes, 'cause if you made one mistake, they had to stop the tape. You had to do a song you never heard before, a chart you never read before, and sit down read the chart, play the song, give it a feel, make it a hit, with no mistakes. That's the big-boy leagues right there.

All Direct

We were all plugged into the monitor speaker and that volume was controlled by the studio, you could only get it so high. I used to play with the speaker behind me and a headset on. I'd take part of the headset off one of my ears, so I could hear the speaker behind me, and in the other head set I could hear the tracks as they were going on tape. If I used some effects it went from my guitar to my effects, straight into the board.

In about 1967, 68 when I got over there, the two drummers, Richard "Pistol" Allen and Uriel Jones, were mic'd with overheads, and they had the kick drum mic'd. You'd have the guitars and a bass, all direct. The other guitar guys before I got there were Robert White, Joe Messina, and Eddie Willis. When I came there were four of us, so three out of the four got to do the session. I could do the funk stuff and the improvised fills like Eddie could, and I could do backbeats. Eddie "Bongo" Brown on congas and Jack Ashford on tambourine were usually standing right in front of me. Earl Van Dyke was playing a big grand piano in one corner and then Johnny Griffith was on organ on the other side of the room. In the overdub room, Jack Brokensha was on vibes. Jack is one of those guys who never gets talked about. He was in The Australian Jazz Quintet. That was the nucleus of what we had.

Ever since "Cloud Nine," one drummer was playing the high hat and the cymbal stuff, and the other drummer was playing the kick and the snare. What you got, which you don't have now, is twelve guys playing together, reading the same arrangement, and they're playing off of each other: that's how you get the feel. Nowadays you got a click track, and you throw in an automated thing doing this or that. You don't have that human interaction of all the musicians playing together.

That's why the Motown records sounded so tight. We had a master rhythm chart of three staves, so we could see all the parts on the charts. We could see the piano parts, I could double bass lines with James Jamerson, because I could read in the bass clef.

I had an opportunity to do one session with Benny Benjamin, who was the original Motown drummer. We did a late-night session at Golden World. It was like 2:00 in the morning. Benny was on salary at Motown. So whenever he came out for a recording session, it had to be a hell of a good payday.

One Sunday at 4:00 in the morning, I did a session at United Sounds Studios. Jamerson and Eddie Willis were on it. There's a knock on the back door and it's Ralph Seltzer, who was "the attorney guy" for Berry Gordy, kind of his right-hand man. He flies in and points at Jamerson and Eddie: "I see you here, Jamerson and Eddie; you are both fined $500 for playing on an outside session."

Hear Me through a Fuzz

I brought all the effects to the party. The first wah-wah pedal on an RnB record was "Cloud Nine" by The Temptations. That won Motown their first Grammy. I've never had a pedal board. In the beginning, I had a Vox Tone Bender for fuzz; I had a Cry Baby wah-wah pedal; and then I had an Echoplex that I used on those sessions. Listen to me on "Ball of Confusion": you can hear me through a fuzz with an Echoplex.

Making Them Horns

Mike Theodore and I were writing a lot of parts for horns and strings, so I said, "Why don't I write parts for guitars like horns and strings?" That was the whole concept for the *Evolution* album. Putting fuzz tones on guitars and making them horns. On "Scorpio," I wrote it out for the horns in sections. Ray Monnette, Joe Padorsik, and I allowed each one of us to put our fuzz tones on it. The three of us played horn parts. I charted it out for the guys. That is why you've got nine guitars on the melody to "Scorpio."

When I finished the *Evolution* album, and Clarence Avant played it for Quincy Jones a year before it came out. Quincy said that "Scorpio" would be the hit off this record.

It's a Free Country

Motown never had me under contract. I was signed as an artist and producer on Sussex Records and Mike Theodore was signed as a producer on Sussex. We were both on a salary. The president of Sussex let me play guitar on other sessions, but Mike and I were not allowed to produce outside sessions. It was all right for me to go out there, but for the guys here, they were pretty much left here.

Bob Babbitt and I were the only Funk Brothers who were free agents. Even in Detroit I was doing a lot of sessions for Holland–Dozier–Holland at night. One day Harry Balk, Head of A&R, called me down to his office downtown. He says, "You're doing all these sessions for us, and we don't want you working for Holland–Dozier–Holland."

I told Harry, "You got me mixed up with the guys you got under this contractual situation. I'm not one of those guys!" He said, "Well, if you keep working for them, we won't call you." I said, "Don't call me. It's a free country." I slammed the door and walked out.

I was in time-out for about two weeks and I could envision Norman Whitfield stewing in the control room. I'm sure he fixed it, because within two weeks I was doing double sessions at Motown every day. No one ever said a word about me working for anybody else.

Musicians Were Stuck

When Motown was here in Detroit, besides me and Bob Babbitt, The Funk Brothers were under contract. They were not allowed to work for anybody else. That's how Berry Gordy kept his sound pure, and it was a regional sound that went global out of Detroit.

But when Berry left, the musicians were stuck here. In LA he was going to be a producer and movie guy. He lost that Motown feel, because everyone he used in LA was playing for everybody else. He didn't have The Funk Brothers anymore. It would have probably been better if he had kept his recording in Detroit and done his other business out in LA. He would have still had that regional sound that no one else could get. CBS & RCA wanted to build studios in Detroit, but they found out Berry had the musicians under contract. They couldn't get them, so they never did.

You Don't Have Enough

I recorded with Wilson Pickett down in Muscle Shoals, Alabama. I played on "Don't Knock My Love" and "Fire and Water." Atlantic Records liked what I did and they hired me to record with Jackie Moore. While I was there, Jerry Wexler wanted to hire me. He said, "I want to hire you to be staff on Atlantic Records in Miami." I answered, "Well, what are we talking about?" He gave me a figure and I said, "You don't have enough money to hire me to come down here and work for you."

JIM KELTNER

Jim Keltner grew up in Tulsa, Oklahoma and moved to Los Angeles when he was 13. He worked at a music store called Berry and Grassmueck, where he taught snare drum. Incidentally, David Lindley taught banjo and Gary Foster taught clarinet there. Keltner got his break in the studio from Gary Lewis, Leon Russell, and Hal Blaine. Today he remains one of the most in-demand studio drummers.

Keltner was a self-described "jazz snob" and would go see Charles Lloyd and Bobby Hutcherson at The Dragonwyck Club in Pasadena. He played jazz gigs with Gabor Szabo and John Handy, and even recorded double drums with Shelly Manne on a John Klemmer project. But he realized at a certain point that the thing that he enjoyed most was playing on records: in the studio. He has played on numerous albums and earned many gold records.

Keltner's credits include Delaney & Bonnie, Bob Dylan, Ringo Starr, John Lennon, Eric Clapton, and Gary Lewis & The Playboys. In the early 1970s, Gary Kellgren started The Jim Keltner Fan Club, a weekly jam session/party at The Record Plant recording studios that Kellgren owned with Chris Stone.

I have interviewed Keltner four times on the radio: August 2014, July 2015, December 2016, and March 2018. He considers me his resident psychologist. These radio excerpts focus on Keltner's concept of love, how he met Ringo Starr, and the lessons he learned from Levon Helm.

Deals with God

I came straight to LA with my mom and dad when I was 13. I was a baseball player in Tulsa, Oklahoma; that was my passion. We got out here and I started breaking out in hives when I got hot playing baseball or riding my bike up a hill. My whole face would swell up, my ear lobes would get real big, my lips would get real puffy. I looked like a monster, so I would go hide. Then it would be gone in twenty or thirty minutes. One time only, I remember I actually passed out in a barber chair. I was like a B movie monster who turns into this creature and 20 or 30 minutes later he's back to normal. The only other person who witnessed that at the time was my wife; she was my girlfriend at the time.

That was big adversity in my life, because I had to give up sports. I had to give up football and baseball. There's always something good that comes out of adversity. The good thing that came out of it was that I wanted to play drums. I wanted to play music.

I had started in Tulsa a little bit, but then I started getting serious when I couldn't play sports anymore. That was a terrifically adverse time in my life. I prayed so much I got real close to God back in those days.

I was all alone and at night I was very depressed. I made deals with God: 'I won't do this anymore, I won't do that anymore. I'll be a really really good person; just take this away from me.' When I think back to that time now, I feel sorry for that little boy.

Bringing Love into the World

Love to me is what makes everything go 'round. I think love created the universe. If you're an atheist, I respect that. I think we all need to respect how each other feels about certain things in life. But if you say you don't believe in God and have a little daughter or a little son and you look in their eyes, you can't tell me that you don't believe in love.

To me "God is love." I believe, especially at this time in the world with what is going on, it's just insane and we need to hold onto to what love is. We need to realize that there's a heavy struggle going on in the world and I don't think any of us really understands it like we should.

I believe Jackie DeShannon said it perfectly: "What the World Needs Now Is Love." That song still makes me cry every time I hear it.

Little Engine Run

The time I loved playing double drums the most was with Ringo on *The Concert for Bangladesh*. I think that may have been the first time we played. Ringo and I share a heartbeat, and it was because I listened to Beatles records. How could you not listen to Ringo? He was everywhere.

Especially if you're starting to do studio stuff, I wanted to get that sound so badly. When I played with Ringo I told myself, "I'm going to play the high hat very, very little, because that's what made the little engine run in Ringo's playing"—the way he played his high hat. I played as minimal as possible on my high hat. When it would come down with the backbeat, I was right with him all the time. I looked at him and watched him a lot. You listen to the *Bangladesh* record, you won't hear two drums.

Phil Spector was recording that show in the truck. Phil was one of my all-time favorite producers.

I've always told Ringo the reason I think we got together so easily was because I listened to him so much. My time feel was naturally similar to his, which is kind of on the backside.

Jim Gordon has a military feel to playing the drums. It served him well on the records that he played on. His exactness and precision around the drums were always something I wanted to emulate. When I first heard him play I said, "I want to do that." I made it my business to really listen and copy him.

Then I got to know him, and they were pairing us up with double drum stuff. That's when I realized that I didn't want to do that anymore. I was up close and I was thinking, "No, I don't want to play like that. He's doing that already. I want to do what I'm hearing in my head."

On the Mad Dogs and Englishmen tour, Jimmy did most of the work, playing the time. I was playing time with him, but I'd coast a little bit. I'd still be playing the time but I'd coast. When it came time to play fills I'd play a fill. It was appropriate for that band, because Leon Russell wanted it to be kind of wild and loose. He didn't want a studio band. That's what I thought I had to do. I realized later on that it was very fortunate for me to have, early on, learned some technique.

High Hat

My first memory of playing with Chuck Rainey was on "Josie" (from *Aja*). He was sitting right next to me. It was at a little studio called Producers Workshop.

Nowadays everybody's spread out a few feet apart. Either that or you're behind baffles. This particular session, there were a lot of players, but Chuck was right by my high hat.

Trade All My Chops

I ended up at Sammy Davis Jr.'s house, and Levon Helm and I hung out for a couple of days. I would watch The Band play; it was extraordinary. He was playing those old drums and he was playing real interesting patterns on the high hat. He'd pull up his right hand from the high hat as he came down on the snare drum. I thought that was amazing and it sounded different. It took away the sound of the metal with the drum at the same time from the high hat.

Then Levon's singing was just mesmerizing. He's one of the great singers of all time. Some people would call him a stylist, but you could not get enough of his singing on any of the songs.

They all were incredible singers. We were talking a lot, and at one point I said to Levon, "Man, if I could just hit one tom-tom and make it sound in the right spot, the way you do, I would trade all my chops for that." He said, "Oh, no, Jimmy, if I could just play those damn little rolls that you do." I said, "Levon, I'll trade ya."

After that I completely changed as a drummer. It wasn't anything I was really conscious off. It didn't hit me. It just started happening and then I realized, as it was happening, that's what happened. I wasn't interested in playing a lot of stuff anymore like I was.

I was always messing with my chops, trying to get fast and play a lot of different stuff. It just went away. I just kept wanting to hear Levon's feel when I played.

Trying to play like Ringo is very much to the point. What does the song want to do right here? What's the best way to make the song feel, right here? Ringo always had that so together. It was never about technique. After I met Levon, that started the undoing of anything I did with technique. That's what I *thought* I had to do. I realized later on that it was very fortunate for me to have learned some technique early on.

I practiced and took lessons from a teacher, Forest Clark, who was with The LA Philharmonic. He told me what I was doing with my left hand was awful. I wasn't utilizing it at all. I only took a few lessons from him, but it started me on that road and I practiced constantly for a long time to get that down. Then it just became a natural thing for me. As I started doing it, I started playing more and getting infatuated with my chops. It was a good thing that I had all that before I decided to undo it.

Too Many Cooks

Gary Kellgren and Chris Stone created The Record Plant in New York and they did the same thing in LA. I became really close friends with Gary and his wife; we used to have dinner all the time. One night Gary said to me, "Let's do something crazy: let's do jam sessions at The Record Plant." I replied, "Yeah, sure!" He said, "We'll have Sunday-night jam sessions and we'll call them The Jim Keltner Fan Club." I responded, "Oh, no, no, no, no, no. You can't call it that." It just felt wrong.

I couldn't stop him from doing it, and it actually worked. Everybody started showing up. John Lennon and his girlfriend May Pang came into town and were having dinner with Richard Perry. Perry said, "Hey, Keltner's having jam sessions down at The Record Plant." John replied, "Really? Let's go down there." He happened to come that night Danny Kortchmar was down there. Danny's a brilliant producer; he made all those Don Henley records.

Kootch brought a song. He said, "Hey, Jimmy, check this out." The name of the song was "Too Many Cooks." I flipped out.

"Where do you find this stuff?"

We decided we were going to work on it the next week. In the meantime, Mick Jagger had called and heard about the song. I told him we were going to work on it, and he showed up. I think he heard it the first time that night—that's how bad Jagger is.

Mick's singing the song, Jack Bruce was playing bass—a stellar cast of people. John being there said, "I'm going to produce this record." John Lennon and Richard Perry are producing Mick Jagger singing "Too Many Cooks"! It was an amazing night. That was the peak of The Jim Keltner Fan Club.

JOE SAMPLE

Joe Sample grew up in the 5th Ward in Houston, Texas. The mayor of his town would not allow Chicago blues to be heard on the radio. Joe spent many a night jamming with Wilton Felder, Wayne Henderson, Hubert Laws, and Stix Hooper, generating their own Gulf Coast sound before hitting the touring circuit as The Nighthawks.

Upon relocating to Los Angeles, Joe helped form the band known as The Crusaders. That exposure led him into the LA studio scene, where he played on thousands of recordings, including Blue Mitchell, Bobby Hutcherson, Donald Byrd, Joni Mitchell, Hugh Masekela, and Henry Mancini. Joe passed away in September 2014.

I did two interviews with Joe: March and December 2012. We talked about the Houston Sound, lessons with Wes Montgomery, how to develop your own individual sound, and how music has become louder, lacking dynamics.

The Sound God Gave You

The common question in the early 1950s was "Who is going to take over where Charlie Parker left off?" That to me is just plain stupid: you can't take over where Charlie Parker left off. Miles Davis even said it. He would talk about the saxophonists in his day imitating Charlie Parker. When all of the saxophone players began to imitate Charlie Parker, then all of a sudden you had something known as Bebop. What Miles was saying was, "Charlie Parker was creating those notes instantly. He hadn't been hearing anyone playing those notes. That was his choice of notes that was coming from his inspirational being." Then everybody thinks, "That's what jazz is. Imitate Charlie Parker and you are playing jazz."

The one thing I think everyone was missing, and certainly isn't here today: not only did I hear Charlie Parker, I heard James Moody, I heard Coleman Hawkins. Everybody had their own particular style. Sonny Stitt came along and they said he was going to be the one to take over where Charlie Parker left off. To me that was all madness: you can't take up where Charlie Parker left off. I could never understand the concept of that. I wish someone had taken up where Paul Desmond left off.

I never wanted to sound like anyone. Yes, I know I was influenced by Oscar Peterson, by Duke Ellington, by Count Basie, by Horace Silver, by Fats Waller, by the boogie woogie piano players of the 1940s. I noticed when I would sit at the piano and play, I didn't play like that. I had this peculiar style that was coming out of me that I didn't like. Then I figured out, "Idiot, that's the sound God gave you." It wasn't until I was around 30 years old that I began to recognize, "Hey, wait a minute, this is what I'm supposed to do." I have a unique style of music and it came out in *Rainbow Seeker* and *Carmel*. Even with The Crusaders' "Put It Where You Want It."

A lot of musicians would come and say to me, "Why are you playing this rock and roll?" I would say, "This is RnB and African American music. Why are you calling this rock and roll? That's something the British brought back in. That's a name that the white industry gave to this music."

Cymbalism

What I have noticed with the drummers of today—they could be in their fifties—is they don't know what cymbals are and don't realize all of the different colors of the cymbals. I get a feeling of drummers that want to play cymbals loud. They do not understand the beauty of the cymbals, and to me that's where it all comes from. It's the cymbal beat, not necessarily the drum. It's certainly not a loud backbeat. It's not loud drums, it's tap dancing on the cymbals.

The tap dancers I saw in the black theaters as a kid in the forties, they would have film shots of the dancers. You could hear the footwork of the dancers. It was very exciting. It was a symbol of America's rhythm, its swing.

All of music is swing, and where does swing come from? West Africa. Everything is based on forms of three. What I hear today with cymbal playing is one volume with one tone. They have no idea of the tonal beauty of the cymbals.

There was a legendary drummer who taught at Berklee named Alan Dawson. I wish Alan was still alive to teach every drummer what America's rhythm is. Not just America's rhythm but what rhythm is. What the sound of music is. The beauty of the cymbals. That's gone, and if that's the first thing to go, how do we expect anyone else to swing?

I think about being in the Fifth Ward of Houston at Wilton Felder's mother's living room. There was a spinet piano in there. We weren't even known as The Crusaders at that time. We were rehearsing in her living room in 1954–55. There were no amplifiers in that room, but you can believe we were groovin'. You don't need an amplifier to groove.

Whitney Houston's performance of the National Anthem at the Super Bowl is one of the all-time greatest performances of any vocalist ever. The woman was in a stadium. Do you know what she did? As the song came to end and was getting louder, she became softer. Then at the very end she drove it home. She used her powerful voice and reached up and grabbed those high notes with the greatest of ease.

Circus Tent

In the black community, whether it started in church or it started in the neighborhood, all the ingredients of African American music, and American music also, were always part of the lives of all the musicians.

In my neighborhood I grew up in a Creole Catholic Church and I heard the typical music you would hear in a Catholic Church. I was at Mass on Sundays. I was an altar boy at one point. I was in Mass for one hour and then I would go home, and on the way home I would pass by ten Black Baptist churches. All my friends, if they weren't Baptist, they were African Methodist. They put on this gig outside my parents' home that was Rhythm and Blues and Gospel/Soul. It was all mixed in there. They were some form of the

Christian Church. A black neighborhood had many, many, many denominations. I heard gospel all day long.

In front of my house was a vacant field, and every summer the holy rollers, the sanctified people, would put a tent there. It was a World War II circus tent, and maybe they could get 40 people in there. It was stifling hot. They had a band, I don't know if they had a piano in there, but they had guitars and banjos, and they conducted their music. It was all based on the pentatonic scale.

When you talk about the pentatonic scale today, who is using the pentatonic scale more than anyone? It's the white girls singing in today's RnB and Pop market. That pentatonic scale has now reached into the white market. I can't remember the names of the girls, but they're usually blond, hot, and sexy, and they do the melismas. They hit the high notes. And all of that is based on the pentatonic scale, which in the old days was called "moaning."

Somehow the Sunshine

The Crusaders all left for Los Angeles at the same time. We left Houston together in June 1958. I was 19 and we all lived in a caravan. My mother said, "If you're going out there, I haven't seen my cousins in years and years. I'm coming with you!" My sister said, "Well, if momma's going and our brother's going, then I'm going too." Once we got in Los Angeles, we rented a house and I knew they were not going back to Houston.

They called my father and said, "Sell the house and meet us out here." My father was so angry, but he did it. He was having all kinds of aches and pains. Somehow the sunshine of Southern California healed his body.

Now that I'm living back in Houston, I know how my father felt. My doctor said, "Joe, you never should have left Southern California."

Dog du jour

In 1968, the Crusaders had a gig at a bar in Cleveland. The piano had only three notes in tune. I saw this church organ over in the corner. I pulled it out and began playing it.

I told the guys later, "I can't do this anymore." I felt as if I was wasting my life. I explained, "All you guys have your horns: you have your trombone, you have your saxophones, you have your drums and your cymbals. What do I have? Dog du jour."

All I Saw Was Blue

I had written a piece for the NDR Big Band in Hamburg, Germany. They asked me to create something for them in 2008. I remember I began working on creating a concept of music concerning slavery. The inspiration came to me when I was staying and performing in the US Virgina Islands Jazz Festival in St. Croix. While there, for the first time in my life, I felt what a slave must have felt. When I got to the top of St. Croix, all I saw was blue and I was standing in the middle of the site where the slaves had processed sugar cane. Instantly I felt that there was no escape. It just hit me, "How did the slave live like this?" He knew he could never run away, because there was that blue ocean out there.

DANNY KORTCHMAR

Guitarist Danny Kortchmar started his career with James Taylor and The Flying Machine in New York in the late 1960s. At that time, he was introduced to Peter Asher and Carole King, who taught him how to play to the song and find guitar parts that fit the song.

In order to grow in life, you need to push yourself out of your comfort zone and learn to communicate with people on the bandstand. For my guest this translated into being part of the quadrangle known as The Section. This fearsome foursome of Craig Doerge, Leland Sklar, Russ Kunkel, and Kortchmar were all trying to grow musically. They found the perfect tonic by listening to each other, building to a crescendo and then releasing back into the ozone in a cosmic sea of extrapolation and forward motion. They became one of the most in-demand studio bands for James, Carole, Jackson Browne, Warren Zevon, and Linda Ronstadt.

Upon moving to the West Coast, he continued his career in the studio as a session player and then as a producer for the likes of Don Henley. He wrote the music for Cheech and Chong's film *Up in Smoke*.

Among these excerpts include Danny's view on how albums are crafted and put together, the role of the studio musician, the first time he met Jim Keltner, and how not to wank on the bandstand (in other words, say what you need to say and get out).

She Believed in Me

Carole King was seminal in my ability to play songs. I would play on all of her demos. She and Gerry Goffin were making demos of all the tunes they wrote. For some reason she believed in me and she kept calling me into these demo sessions. That's how I learned to play on records. She's a musical genius without any question: not just as a song writer, but as a producer and arranger.

Myddle C

James Taylor and I had The Flying Machine. It was made up of two electric guitars, bass, and drums. We were playing at The Night Owl Cafe down on 3rd Street and MacDougal. We managed to hold on to our gig for a long time. One of the things that drove James crazy about TNOC was that there were no monitors. He had to sing way louder then he should have had to, to get over the sound of the band.

A lot of bands would come through there and some of them were really good. Bands were constantly auditioning to play there. One of the bands that played there I had already heard about: they were called The Myddle Class. It turned out that Carole King and Gerry Goffin had signed them to their little label, Tomorrow. Charlie Larkey was in TMC; he and I became good friends. He was hanging out in the Village, and after both of our bands broke up, we wound up in The Fugs.

Shoot for the Stars

In my opinion the thing that John McLaughlin and John Coltrane had in common was that they were both really trying to get high. They started out using drugs and then went to a much higher plane, a spiritual plane. As I watched McLaughlin play, he was shooting for the stars. He was trying to get to a place that's beyond anything that can be described: a very high place. I think with Coltrane it was the same thing. You listen to Coltrane's stuff when he went modal, it's so absolutely riveting. It takes you to a place every time. It still does; it's real extraordinary.

Me and my pals used to go into the Village all the time. We'd go to the Half Note and The Five Spot and all these groovy jazz clubs like Slugs, where I saw Cecil Taylor and the original Coltrane Quartet. Awesome, really long, unbelievable solos that Trane was playing. I'll never forget it.

Spin Doctors

All the records we, The Section, made, including Carole King's *Tapestry* and James Taylor, we were all in the room together. Everyone was in the same room playing at the same time, so we quickly learned to play together. Playing on *Tapestry* and Taylor's *Sweet Baby James*: that lit us all up.

I was taught to play in the studio by some very astute fellows, namely Peter Asher, Lou Adler, and Carole. They always brought me back to the song: what's best for the song? Don't play over the melody; play something that's going to help. This was before you could amplify an acoustic guitar, so James is playing to the mic. We're all walking on eggshells. Keep it down to a level where James' guitar and vocal can be heard. We were all sitting down close to each other. Peter Asher made the template for that music when he produced *Sweet Baby James*. That's how we learned to play together. That record and the next one, *Mud Slide Slim and the Blue Horizon*. That's where Russ, Lee, and I learned to play that music.

We got into the studios from that. Peter Asher was the first producer to put the names of the accompanists on the albums. The Wrecking Crew is not well known, because they played on many records but they weren't listed. These records came along, and we were kind of the next generation of the Wrecking Crew. Because Peter and Lou were putting the names of the musicians on the albums, we got recognition. We started getting a lot of calls, especially Russ and Lee.

That sounds like an obvious thing, but it isn't. Very, very few records are made like that anymore. They're mostly made piecemeal, one part at a time. When I was producing a lot of records in the 80s and 90s, I would put all the guys in the room. I produced a Spin Doctors album where they were all in the room together. I never really got into doing one part at a time.

As far as analog to digital, I think that's overrated. If Tom Dowd had had Pro Tools, working on all those early Aretha Franklin records, he would have absolutely loved it. The analog sound comes to the signal, not where it ends up. Really good engineers know how to mic stuff. They know how to mic a drum kit and mic a room that has four or five guys in it. At that point the difference between recording to tape or Pro Tools is minuscule. More is made out of it than is there. It's about the chain: the mics and preamps that you use. Again, it very much has to do with guys in a room. If you don't have guys in a room together, you're not going to get that sound. It's what happens when everyone plays together.

All my favorite guitar players growing up were like that, too. Steve Cropper, Curtis Mayfield, Cornell Dupree, David T. Walker: all those guys knew how to set up a song. Everybody else was listening to lead guitar, and I was listening to these guys. To me, Steve Cropper's playing on those Stax/Volt Records is the essence of how you play a song. You have to serve the song.

I have a huge ego. But when I have to find the right part for a song, that upstages my ego. When I was playing with James and Carole, I was jamming all the time, every day. I was able to play solos, turn up, and play louder.

When you hear a song like "You've Got a Friend," forget your ego. That's a great song. All I try to do is find some way to help tell the story.

Holiday Inn

The song "Shaky Town" came from trucker' dialogue on CB Radio. CB Radio had its own language, and because I was touring so much, I wanted to write a song that was a combination of the guys who drove our gear around and the musicians.

The drivers who drove the trucks that took our stuff hither and yon, and the musicians themselves: I tried to have reference points for both of those groups. Jackson Browne recorded this song on his *Running on Empty* album. That whole album was done on the road. At one point in the tour I played the song for Jackson. I thought that maybe the tune would fit in, but I really didn't think he was going to jump on it. He did. He told me, "We've got to record it!" I said, "Let's do it!"

We were at a Holiday Inn and they rented a room and piled up all the furniture and took it out. They brought in a set of drums. The next room over was where the 24-track was. They set up mics. It was me, Russell, Leland Sklar, and David Lindley on lap steel. We recorded the entire thing in a Holiday Inn motel room.

Out of the Question

Going off on 20-minute solos is as boring as horseshit. Get in and out. What about the groove? We're about getting people to tap their feet and shake their ass. None of us are John Coltrane, not the best of us. Nobody wants to hear 20-minute solos, and I have no intention of playing one tune for 20 minutes, that's out of the question. It's a more groove-oriented thing than a look-at-me-solo kind of thing.

Nobody ever had to tell me that, because I was never "Just wanking it." That's the way I was trained by the people I learned how to play music from: Peter, Lou Adler, and Carole. With those guys you play an eight-bar solo or a sixteen-bar solo and get out. I'm not a jazz musician nor am I a guitar soloist.

I've played in the ensemble and that's always been my joy, my delight. What I go for is soul, feeling. Musicians never want it to end. They don't want to be part of a moment that only lasts a few years and goes away.

Musicians are all about love and the musicians I know—and I know a lot of them—absolutely love each other. They love playing together, they glow, and I do, too. It's a profound situation to play music with other people. It creates a bond, especially when you've been playing and listening since you were 10. It was a lifetime thing with all of us. Then, now, and forever, I am interested in a musical conversation.

If you go to Berklee or one of the heavy-duty music schools to be a shredder, to play solos? Good luck with that. If you think anybody's going to pay to hear you shred, you're probably wrong. There's maybe five guys that people will pay to listen to them play fast. I was taught to play parts on records that helped the singer and the song and the producer. That seems to be a dying art, now that you rarely hear guitars on recordings at all anymore. Where does the guitar fit in now? I'm not really sure. I'm hoping that guys recognize and rediscover what great ensemble guitar playing is. I don't know if that will happen or not.

Adjusting to the Zeitgeist

In the 80s, every hair metal band and every song that came out was verse, A section, B section, chorus, A section, B section, chorus, guitar solo. Every song had a guitar solo in it.

I realized that people were going to get sick of these stupid ass "Les-Paul-through-a-Marshall guitar solos" over and over again. People get tired of everything, and sure enough that's what happened. Nirvana came along: no guitar solos, just rhythm and songs. Then the technology came along and people got interested in making whole records on their laptop. I think a lot of people who were thinking about becoming guitar players ended up adjusting to the Zeitgeist, which had more to do with programming.

What I've been working on for a long time is tightening up the gap between what's called rhythm guitar playing and lead guitar playing. I don't think those need to be two different things.

This has been going on for years. You bang away on your rhythm guitar and you wait for your solo. When your solo comes, you kick on your overdrive and blast away. You kick the thing off, then and you go back to "Strum-a, a-strum, a-strum."

As a producer I got very impatient dealing with certain people who had never made records before and would go out there and screw around for a while. A lot of the teeny-bopper pop music you hear on the radio now is all canned, reproduced, manufactured, put through the cheese grater. I don't think there are many records made today where you're hearing an actual performance.

Pro Tools is a tool, it's not the villain itself, and it's a matter of who's driving. If you have a great vocal performance, you may have to fix one thing or two things, sure. Use Pro Tools as a basic digital editing process to do that. The problem comes before you ever get to Pro Tools. It comes down to who is an artist. There's only ten guys producing all these records. Basically, how the songs get written, it's a track, then they get a singer who can sing it in that key.

I don't understand why Kim Kardashian doesn't make records. Who not? It doesn't matter whether she can sing or not, she's famous. We have a different paradigm today compared with what was going on before. Producers and record companies probably feel that there's no room for a quiet part in a song. People will turn it off and go listen to something else. It's all got to be in your face all the time. Ballads, funk, hard rock, doesn't matter: pumped up, mastered so that it's one dynamic level. It works for the people who love it, I guess.

Music does not run the culture any longer. You don't sit with your earphones on and listen to a whole James Taylor record and go, "God, he's talking about my life." I think most young people, when they're listening, are multi-tasking. They're listening but they're also texting or tweeting—doing something else along with listening. Music is not one of the most important things in our culture. It has become insignificant as a driving force in our culture.

How They Can Help

Russell Kunkel is a finesse drummer, he's not a pounder. The first thing Russ does is listen: What am I saying? What's the song? What does the artist have to say? What's my role here? How can I help? What can I do that's going to help the song and help the band and especially help the singer.

Those are his first, second and third thoughts. How he uses the cymbal is based on what he thinks is going to help. Going from the high hat to the ride cymbal, when he does it, how he does it, how much power he puts into it—are all based on what context he's in.

He, Jim Keltner, Rick Marotta: they pay serious attention to their sound and what they have to offer and how they can help. Everyone has a different approach, but that approach is always based on the context they're in.

Including Me

Jim Keltner was and is a great friend. One of the greatest musicians in the world and definitely from his generation.

We were doing a session around 1973 at United Western, which was one of the great studios back in the day. I knew about Keltner. I'd heard about him. I thought of him as a jazz drummer, because he played with Charles Lloyd and Gabor Szabo and those cats doing LA jazz.

He always wears his shades and he looks really cool. First time we're playing together and he's behind the baffle. I can see him but just from the chest up. He's playing but I can't really see his hands move. Then I put the phones on and there's this incredible sound coming from his drums. I realized I was entering a whole other area.

So I'm playing my rhythm guitar doing the thing that I do, and Keltner says to the engineer, "Can you move this baffle out of the way, so I can see this guitar player?" He's pointing right at me. Right there we became great friends.

His kit is so beautifully tuned; it's just so musical. His chops, his sound, comes from the way he hits those drums as well as his aesthetic and overall approach. All musicians are different for that very reason. The guys from the era that you're talking about all had a sound, including me.

LELAND SKLAR

Bassist Leland (Lee) Sklar has brought his sense of elasticity to the studio, locking the groove, no matter how much glad bashing is going on around him. He has contributed to thousands of albums over the course of his career, from bluegrass with Byron Berline to heroin rock with James Taylor or cowboy country tunes with Leon Russell and Willis Alan Ramsey. Lee could fit right inside some Spanish swing or white-man gospel or funky blues. He came up during a time in the record industry when musicians were recognized for their craft—so much so that they gave cats like Lee identities for their prowess.

Lee knows his instrument but he has feeling: the feeling of love that exists when everyone is listening and playing off of each other. This was the brotherhood that he came from. Learning experientially, getting the charts 20 minutes before the session, and playing their tails off. He is in the same master bass discussion as Monk Montgomery, Wolfgang Meltz, and James Jamerson.

I have interviewed Lee five times on my radio program: July 2014 (twice), August 2014, November 2014, and February 2017.

These excerpts include: the story behind the making of Billy Cobham's *Spectrum*, how the recording industry has been truncated from concept albums to EPs, what it means to say "yes" to a recodring date, how musical talent has to be cultivated in order to bloom, his relationship with Bill Graham, and how he tries to bring a positive vibe to any recording situation.

Love

What it really comes down to is opening your heart, being accessible and vulnerable, so you can run with all the emotions. I don't look at love as an intellectual thing. It's a far more visceral, gut-level feeling.

Filmation

I think the busiest time for the classic studio musician was through the entire 1970s into the 80s. I still feel really blessed that I'm working all the time still, at this point.

There were long periods of time when we were doing, on average, three or four sessions a day for five or six days a week for months and months on end. It was a core of people who were doing the bulk of it, in the way the guys from The Wrecking Crew were doing it from the end of the 50s through the 60s.

It was the time of record companies and a lot of artists were signed. The studios were cranking around the clock, so there was so much work to be done. Nowadays albums aren't being made the way they were. People might only be able to go in and do singles or EPs; it's not a full-on album project. Labels are a diminishing aspect of the business, because everybody's looking for Indie work.

But the intensity of the studio work was quite remarkable back in that period. It was quite ferocious where we could be showing up to do an 8:00 am movie call at 20th Century Fox and work until noon. Then I'd be working 1pm–4pm and then 5pm–9pm. Sometimes we would go past midnight. There were times when we'd go into the studio and it was dark out and we'd come out and it was dark out. We would never even see the sun. We would be doing a hard rock session and then turn around and be working with The Archers or some contemporary Christian group. We used to do all the Filmation cartoons, such as *Jabberjaw* and *Groovy Goolies*. I remember one time we were sitting around trying to figure out what we were doing, and Ted Knight walked in and we did a film score called *Hi Guys*, which was at the height of the Mary Tyler Moore show. We did stuff like "Pinball Wizard" and "Blueberry Hill."

There were many different groups, but for the Filmation shows a lot of times it would be Mike Baird on drums, Don Randi might be playing keyboard, sometimes David Foster when he first came to town. There were rhythm sections that would end up doing different kinds of projects.

I was in a band in 1967 called Group Therapy. Mike Post produced us, and it was during that time when we weren't allowed to play on our own record. I remember going into the studio and sitting on the other side of the glass and watching The Wrecking Crew make our record. At the time Post had been working with Mason Williams and was the musical director for the Andy Williams Show. Somehow we hooked up with him and he invited us over to United Artists Studios. We were there two nights. The first night Hal Blaine played drums and the next night Earl Palmer played drums. Jim Gordon played percussion, and Michel Rubini, Mike Melvoin, and Larry Knechtel were the three keyboard players. Dennis Budimir was on guitar, Carol Kaye was on electric bass, and Bobby West was playing upright. I'm looking through the glass and saying, "Holy crap, look at these people." Never in a million years did I think I would become a studio musician. That was in 1967, and by 1970 I was working with these people every day.

Self-Perpetuating Piece of Machinery
Everybody has a point of pride in what they are doing. When your phone rings, you have two options. You can say yes or no. If you say yes, it comes with obligation. You really need to step up to the plate. I'll go do a session for somebody and I've got to do a completely different session the next day. The session I did for the guy that day, though, might be his only shot at the business. If this isn't successful, he's out and has to look for a new life. I'm going on to something else and something else and something else. I feel a sense of obligation that if I say yes and show up, I'm going to do the best job I possibly can. Be as engaged and involved as I possibly can. When I walk out the door, this guy's got the best thing going, and out of that he'll get more work. It really is a self-perpetuating piece of machinery.

It's always funny to me, you would work on album projects, and they'd be nickel-and-diming every player on the dates, yet they would drop a quarter of a million dollars to do the video. This didn't happen overnight. It's like a disease that eats away at you over the course of many years, as compared with dropping you on the spot. When I go to The NAMM Show, I see all these young players that are just monsters, and they're so hungry to do what guys like me did. The real sad part is the reality that the opportunity to do what we did really doesn't exist the way it did. It's not to say you can't be successful in the music business, and there's people every day that wind up signing record deals or have some song that becomes the darling of the moment. Artist development doesn't exist anymore. I don't want to discourage people from pursuing it at all, because it's essential for our society that musicians and artists be here to counterbalance the lack of soul that seems to be going on, on a daily basis, in this world right now.

Blocks of Foam Rubber

When I played with Herb Pedersen and Country Gazette, I'd bring one of my older electric basses. I'd stick some foam in it, to deaden the sound. I got a few tricks I do just to give as much variety to a single instrument that I possibly can. I carry different blocks of foam rubber with me.

I remember Bob Babbitt once talked about buying a cheap kitchen sponge and cutting it into little pieces. What he would tend to do, rather than shoving foam underneath, between the string and the body, he would have these little blocks and put one between the G and the D strings and another one between the A and the E strings.

I do that all the time now. I just did a project with Steve Tyrell where he was doing songs in tribute to the Brill Building. One of the songs I thought would sound better if it had a "dead sound." I normally play with stainless flatwounds. All of a sudden it sounded like I had old La Bella flatwounds on it.

The Broken String

Billy Cobham called me up and said he got a record deal and he wanted to know if I could come to New York to work on his album *Spectrum*. I said, "Geez are you kidding? I would love to." Other than two tracks done with a big band—Ron Carter played bass on those two tracks—all the rest of the tracks we did in two days. It's pretty much one or two takes of each track. They were all cut live, no overdubs.

There's a track called "Taurian Matador," and Jan Hammer and Tommy Bolin trade licks back and forth. At one point if you're listening to the record, you hear Tommy play his notes "Errr, errr, errr, brak." He broke his E string right in the middle of his solo, and he kept on playing and finished played the head and finished the song. They never went in and fixed it, so the broken string is on the album.

I had known Tommy since he was in a band called Zephyr. When I was in Wolfgang, we did some work together. Our LA manager managed both of us. We would go out and open for War. I had known Tommy a long time and I had no idea he was going to be the guitar player when I walked into Electric Lady Land.

One of the reasons that *Spectrum* has stood the test of time is that Tommy and I were really rock players. I was not a fusion jazz player. It was that kind of amalgamation of Billy and Jan bringing their jazz fusion, and Tommy and I bringing our rock fusion aspect to it. It took on this whole other vibe from The Headhunters and Mahavishnu Orchestra and Return to Forever. All those guys were jazz fusion guys.

On Wolfgang

When I was in college, I was real tight with a few of the guys from Pacific Gas and Electric, which was a band that emanated out of the area. The whole spirit of that area was beautiful. I remember being on the Chitlin Circuit and we'd go up Mandrakes to play a gig.

We had a manager named Bruce Gladner whose company was Shady Management, and my God, if ever name was prophetic, that was it. He also had the band Zephyr, which included Tommy Bolin.

Bruce had an affiliation with Bill Graham, and so because of that my band Wolfgang became closer to Bill and to David Rubinson, who was a major record producer up there. We cut a few demos that have never seen the light of day. A few 45s.

Bill's real name was Wolfgang, and we thought, "There's no better way to suck up to our new manager than to name our band after him."

It was about a year later that I met James Taylor, and we did a lot of work at the Berkeley Community Theatre, and suddenly I was involved with Bill on a much more regular basis. Plus we closed out the Fillmore East; we were the next-to-last act. So I got to be real tight with Bill.

It brings me back to, "Why did he have to get in that helicopter?" Bill died in a helicopter crash. There was a car waiting to take him from Concord, but he needed to get back. The weather got real bad, and I think they hit power lines. What a loss.

When we played at The Greek Theatre, Bill would always do the most outrageous backstage events. We'd show up and there would be huge spreads and Hawaiian themes. He was a master of ceremonies; just loved to be in the middle of everything.

Bill loved the musicians but he loved the audience more. I remember we went to a gig just to hang out. I won't mention the band's name, but they had finished their set, and the audience was just screaming, going nuts, wanting an encore. The band wasn't really acting on it. They were sitting back, digging themselves. I see Bill take them by the scruff of their neck and push them back out to the stage yelling, "Get out there!" More than anything he wanted the crowd to have a great experience. He really believed in that relationship between artist and audience. He wouldn't tolerate any BS from anyone. You read stuff about people disparaging him. He was a task master in an incredibly positive way, and his priority was always to make the show and the scene better.

RANDY BRECKER

Growing up in Philly, Randy Brecker was immersed in a thriving music scene and inspired by Miles Davis, Dizzy Gillespie, and Clifford Brown.

He studied in David Baker's jazz program at Indiana University, where he collaborated with Booker T. Jones. Returning to the East Coast, Randy became a first-call session player. While playing in the studios he was also part of the original Blood Sweat & Tears. He left them to join Horace Silver and gained bandstand experience with Bennie Maupin, the bassist John B. Williams, and Billy Cobham.

When his brother Michael came of age, Randy formed the iconic jazz rock outfit known as Dreams with him. He opened his own club called Seventh Avenue South in the Village, where all the cats could come and lay out after a day in the studios.

I had a chance to interview Randy on my radio show twice, in March and May 2017, and a Facebook Live interview in December 2017.

These excerpts include: playing with dynamics, the loft music scene of the mid-1960s, what happened after he hadn't seen his brother play after four years, how his brother's death affected him, and his family's musical heritage.

Parallel Realities

Playing music is seen as a "musician's gift to the world." We're supposed to hand out our music for free, and that's not in sync with what I was brought up to do. As a player, I don't think people have respect for how much time and work goes into practicing your instrument and trying to write music. It's not fun in that respect, and we want to be paid for it.

There are parallel realities going on in pop music: you do have machines practically involved in every almost every record you hear. Even the stuff coming out of Nashville, although it seems that's where most of the musicians have settled. They're playing on the newer country scene, and I like to hear that. On the general pop music scene and urban scene, it's mostly just hip hop machines with a rapper and one or two guys scratching. Even when you see a lot of groups on TV, they're kind of faking it. It's very sad for me; I like to see a band play.

One Day I Did

I came to New York in September 1966 and got sucked into so many scenes because there was so much work around in different genres. I was trying to finish school, but there was so much work around: studio, live, Dave Liebman's loft and Chick Corea's. We would play for hours just off the top of our head; the next place you'd go was a straight-ahead bebop session. One day I did a rehearsal with Ornette Coleman and a record date with Johnny Cash, playing mariachi trumpets. It was after "Ring of Fire": he was trying to recreate that hit. You had to be familiar with a lot of different styles of music if you wanted to work.

A Third Dimension

I played with a lot of different styles of groups. There were organ trios, and there were always lots of dynamics with the organ trios because the drummer had to play soft enough to be able to hear organ bass, which isn't even as carrying as an acoustic bass. There was always a lot of air in the music in that context. A lot of space for horns to develop, and good organ players always had a sense of dynamics with the pedals and the volume pedal.

The acoustic jazz band was always the same thing: dynamics were built into the music. If you were going to repeat the melody, you played it a little louder the second time. If there was a fade, you would start the fade softer and let it build up, so it just wasn't an *ff* dynamic all the time.

Dave Holland told me this years ago: "Listen from the bottom up." Good drummers didn't want the bass drum to get in the way of the bass, so they didn't rely on it as much. Everybody wanted to hear the bass.

I always use Elvin Jones as the perfect example. He could bash his butt off, if he wanted to, but there was always a sense of dynamics and air and space in his music. If a guy played too loud, he'd snarl at the guy. One time I remember Frank Foster was playing in the right dynamic and Steve Grossman came in too loud. Elvin gave him that snarl, and Steve got soft quick.

If you hear early Charlie Parker records and Miles and Dizzy, there was always that air and space in the music. My father was a piano player and bebopper. When I was younger, I got to hear these guys live, mostly at a place called The Red Hill Inn in Pennsauken, New Jersey. I heard Dizzy there several times and Miles. Miles playing with a Harmon mute. Just think of that these days!

Everybody had to play soft. There wasn't any amplification. You had to hear yourself. Philly Joe Jones: there was always space. Paul Chambers: you could always hear him. And there was natural dynamics in the band. When Miles put in a Harmon mute, it was a great sound. And the secret of the way he played it was he played it softly. He didn't overblow the Harmon mute, so he got a nice firm round sound. These days you hear guys put in a Harmon mute and they can't hear themselves, so the first thing they do is overblow and it sounds shrill.

We learned dynamics because we needed them. We couldn't play full volume every night. We had microphones, we didn't have monitors, and in loud bands you were easily overshadowed. There was constant talk among players: when to hit it, when to rest, when to play soft. It was part of the lexicon, especially with Horace Silver. He always talked about dynamics. And when you heard his band or Art Blakey's band, you always heard dynamics. That's what gave the music a third dimension. People weren't just playing at the top volume, "at 11" as they said in *This is Spinal Tap*. It was just part of the acoustic music scene and it was also part of the better jazz rock scene.

Light My Fire

I was away at Indiana University when my brother really developed his style. When I left home, Michael was in 9th grade and had just taken five or six years of clarinet lessons, which he never really took to, although that gave him a great foundation, whether he knew it or not.

He discovered Cannonball Adderley. I was taking lessons with David Baker and I would send him some exercises. I didn't really hear him play for the next three years, until I joined Horace Silver in 1967.

In 1968 we were playing for two weeks at the famed Plugged Nickel in Chicago. By then Michael had already had a year at Indiana University under his belt himself, and had his own jazz-rock band with the great trumpet player Randy Sandke. Their main claim to fame was getting kicked out of the Notre Dame Jazz Festival for playing jazz-rock instead of "jazz." It made *Downbeat*: group disqualified at Notre Dame Jazz Festival because they played a jazz-rock version of 'Light My Fire.'" Ray Brown and Oliver Nelson, the judges, hated it and took umbrage against the group.

Michael and Randy were living down the street and doing some gigs around Chicago, so we decided to have a jam session. I brought Billy Cobham and Bennie Maupin over to their crash pad. Michael played and our jaws just dropped. I had never heard a saxophone played like that before. He was a diamond in the rough. He wasn't fully developed yet, but he had the chops. He had this unique way of uniting Trane with King Curtis and Junior Walker. He was already Michael Brecker, and I had missed that developmental period 'cause I wasn't home.

Michael wasn't a natural leader. But when he played, he took charge of the whole bandstand. He never felt he was able to do his own solo records till he was 38. He was filled with such humility, he never thought he was ready to go out on his own.

We All Looked up

Carl Shroeder, the pianist with Sarah Vaughan in the 1960s and 70s, wasn't afraid to say anything. I remember sitting around with Dave Liebman, Grossman, and Don Alias. Carl stood up and he said, "All you guys do is sit around and talk about Miles Davis," and he was right. We all looked up to Miles and his band and wanted to know what was going to happen next.

That Miles Band with Tony Williams and Ron Carter had total trust in each other. Not only would they break up the time and then come back to it, but they would break up the form and they would go out into left field. At the time I couldn't figure out if they did or didn't know where they were. Part of the time they didn't: they weren't afraid to just take it out there somewhere. They trusted each other musically to find their way back, which is what they did. I always found that fascinating: they weren't afraid to take chances and go to territory where no man has gone before, and then find their way back. Then when we would try to play, we'd try to imitate them.

His Main Inspiration

If my brother's death had been more sudden, it would have been much harder, but we knew it was coming. I remember I was playing a concert in Tennessee and heard from my sister that he was really not doing well and it sounded like the end was imminent. I thought about him through the whole concert and the whole way home. By the time I got home, he had passed already.

It still didn't make it easier, because you're dealing with a whole new level of grief. In the ensuing years I've tried to do what I thought he would want me to do musically, spiritually, and as husband and father, because he measured so high on all those fronts. His demise inspired me to start writing music for the first time in a long time.

My brother was so serious and he worked so hard at his music. His main inspiration was John Coltrane, and I think he continued that tradition by practicing for hours and hours and hours every day. He was never satisfied with his own playing and kept adding to his vocabulary. Usually when you get a little older you tend to slow down a little, and he didn't.

Later in his life he got interested in Bulgarian folk music and studied with Bulgarian musicians and started to write. There's a tradition of Eastern European music that features incredible technique. There's a lot of woodwind music entrenched in the music, particularly in Bulgarian folk music, wedding bands, and virtuosic stuff. I think that caught his ear. Again he reinvented the saxophone. It was completely different from anything he'd done before and anything anybody had ever done before.

Earthly Terms

I'm listening to music all the time, on and off the bandstand. That's really, in a nutshell, how I learned to play. I was playing along with records, sitting around listening deeply to what each guy was doing and how they responded to each other. I listen very intently when I'm improvising, and hopefully playing with guys that are great. The records would feed you ideas, and you could bounce them off each other. That's what really separates the men from the boys: when you get guys who really know how to respond to what's going on, and to the music that's surrounding all of us. You leave earth for a while and just respond to colors and sound. I don't know how to explain it in earthly terms, because you're responding to something without words.

RON TUTT

Born in Texas, Ron Tutt grew up playing Western Swing before getting an audition with Elvis Presley. He won the job and was Elvis's road drummer for years. He recorded with Roy Orbison, The Carpenters, and Lalo Shifrin.

At a certain point Tutt was the most in-demand session drummer in LA. He played on jazz, rock, country, and gospel records. In the mid-70s he was playing live with Jerry Garcia and Elvis. Today he is the drummer for Neil Diamond. He has also worked with Elton John and Cat Stevens.

Among the excerpts included are: how he got his gig with Elvis, being humbled trying to learn reggae music, how he held Legion of Mary together, and having huge elephant ears.

Huge Elephant Ears

You have to be prepared with whatever you do. I played enough kinds of music with enough great musicians in Dallas and in Memphis. With Elvis I had a good amount of confidence that I could do whatever was asked of me. That versatility came in again, no matter what feel of the song he would bring in, whether it was a country feel or an old blues feel or a rock and roll feel or rockabilly. I felt like I could handle it.

That was the beauty and versatility of Elvis' band. We played all that stuff. Same with Garcia: we played so many different genres, so many different styles. It helped to feel good and get comfortable with them. You have to have confidence in yourself that you can do it, without being a big swelling ego thing. You have to know "This is what I do. I hope we hit it off."

I tell young drummers they've got to develop big huge elephant ears. In the case of the bass player, the drummer has to listen to him. It's a marriage: that's why I was fortunate to play with bass player Jerry Scheff. We played on a lot of projects together. Then it was John Kahn and then Reinie Press.

Subdivide

In the jazz world, it's known that slow songs are harder to play than fast ones. Guys are trying to show their chops off, with how fast they can play. The real challenge is to play slow and make it cohesive. You have to subdivide and learn to play in between the notes. It's what you play in between and lay down the pattern that helps keep it together.

I had to learn my role with Garcia. Jerry is such a wonderful player when it comes to the real "passionate ballads," I like to call them. The challenge is to play at a very slow tempo, and you have to subdivide. We never talked about anything, we just played. Jerry felt the songs that way and it's how we felt.

I met those guys, Garcia and Kahn, at Jerry's first recording session in LA. John was looking for a rhythm section mate, and he thought we would do really well together. When I put down my right foot on the bass drum pedal, he was right there every time. He never pushed, he never dragged, he was right with me. We tried to listen to each other a great deal. We never had to talk about anything. It was kind of like a jazz group. All of Legion of Mary's songs have a head, they have an open solo, and everybody plays as much as they want to play, as long as they want to, then you have the ending. No matter what song we were playing, that's the way they all came out.

Color Player

My first paying gig was Western Swing, which is a form of jazz and which is a form of two-beat music, too. I went from that into Dixieland into jazz. As far as drummers are concerned, I appreciated both schools: the bebop and the harder East Coast bop. I was fascinated by the taste of guys like Shelly Manne, Mel Lewis, and Stan Levey (who played with Charlie Parker), and Max Roach.

Much later on I was fascinated by the great reggae bands and artists out of Jamaica. I did a session down in Houston and they had a warehouse full of reggae records that had been made up till that point in time. They were distributing the records and were going out of business. They said, "Take what you want," because they were going to give them away. I grabbed a huge armful of vinyl by The Heptones and shipped it all home. I studied and studied, because reggae music was the first thing that came along to me that was really, really different. It put the drummer in a totally different role, and I wanted to know how to do it. The drummer wasn't really the basic timekeeper anymore; he was like the color player. He played over the top of the guitar or organ. They were laying down a rhythm track, and the drummer would play over the top of that with different little fills and accents. The way the drums were tuned made a difference, too. Those are the authentic styles of reggae.

The Guy's on My Drum Set

I auditioned with Elvis in Las Vegas in 1969. They had been trying out drummers for a few weeks in preparation for Elvis's return to live performing. He hadn't done that in ten years. I got a call from my friend Larry Muhoberac, who said, "I put your name in the hat. Can you come out tomorrow night?" It was a Friday night and they were holding auditions for one more day.

I flew out to LA, came early to the session, and set my drums up. They had kinda of settled on this one guy who had done a lot of Motown dates in LA. He started playing, and you could see the nods of approval from the guys, "We got the drummer. We're cool." I'm sinking lower and lower in my chair thinking, "I came all the way out here, the guy's on my drum set, and I'm not even going to get a chance to play."

About the end of it everybody starts to put their instruments away and Larry goes over to Colonel Parker's table, and I see him pointing over to me, reminding him that he had flown me out here to audition. The Colonel went up to Elvis and said, "You know we got this one other guy who came out from Texas." Begrudgingly you could see everybody taking out their instruments and plugging back in.

We immediately hit it off musically: the attention, the eyes. We could communicate without saying stuff. It worked out pretty good.

BUZZ FEITEN

Buzz Feiten grew up on Long Island, learning to like the sound that emanated from his guitar, before working on his chops. He was playing bass with Elvin Bishop, who hipped Paul Butterfield to Buzz. Butter didn't need a bass player, so he hired Buzz as a lead guitarist. The rest is history. Buzz became a leading session guitarist on both coasts, recording with Stevie Wonder, Don McLean, Gregg Allman, The Rascals, and his own group, Full Moon. Today Buzz is a custom guitar designer in Los Angeles.

Amongst the excerpts included are: Buzz talking about how Elvin Bishop hipped him to Paul Butterfield, being in the studio with Bob Dylan, liking the sound that was coming out of his guitar as opposed to focusing on chops, and how he decided to live a "magical life."

Nothing to Do with Me

I decided a long time ago I wanted to live a magical life. That's up to me, if I lead a magical life or a life of quiet desperation.

Magic, to me, is when people play music together. That's a gift from God. We don't create that. We don't create anything; we're just vehicles or channels. Sometimes God throws a big bucket of talent into somebody and sometimes he doesn't; he gives that person talent in another area. Musical talent is a gift from God, and it's random and you're lucky if you have it. The best you can hope to be is a good proprietor or a good steward of that gift.

I don't try to take credit for making music. If I have talent, I don't take any credit for that. That has nothing to do with me. That's just a gift. I believe God gave people like me a chance to live a magical life, if *they* choose to. That's what it's about for me, man.

If I have talent, I don't take any credit for that. That has nothing to do with me, that's just a gift. Someone walks up to you and gives you a million dollars, then you have the freedom to do a lot of stuff with the money. It's a gift; you didn't earn it.

My Playpen

Something that was beat into me at an early age was to listen to the sounds you make. You have to like the sounds you're making on whatever instrument you're playing. Sometimes I think that gets overlooked or neglected. People are focused on chops and notes and technique, and they forget to listen to the sound they're making. Not everybody of course; there's some fantastically technically brilliant players that also have a great tone. The two things are not mutually exclusive. Sometimes first liking the sounds you're making and then working on your technique is the way to go.

Like most young players, I overplayed. You get carried away, you don't know when to stop.

I started to construct solos with a beginning, a middle, and an end. The "middle period" was a development period that built tension by adding rhythmic complexity, harmonic complexity, by adding a denser volume of notes and then coming to some kind of peak shortly before the ending or at the ending.

Here's my playpen — my playpen is ten feet long and eight feet wide — and I can run around in that playpen, but I have to know where the edge of it is. I've got to know my boundaries.

You get better at it as you do it more. You learn to make a statement and then work your way into more complexity and more intensity. You work your way out of it by finding something that feels emotionally satisfying somewhere towards the end. Then you work your way out of it gracefully through a descending-note pattern. All of this has to be driven by emotions.

Criticize Himself

Paul Butterfield was an incredibly generous cat, musically and personally. He had so much respect for the people that he played with, I almost never heard him say a critical word to anyone. He would criticize himself before he would criticize anybody else. He understood that the way to get the best out of somebody is to let them go. You hired them for a reason; and the one thing you want to do, if you're smart, is let people be who they are, and you're going to get some incredible stuff if they're creative, talented players. Butter knew how to do that. He would encourage people to take long, long solos. He encouraged people to grab a different instrument. I remember some jam sessions where someone would wind up banging on the mic stand with a drumstick, but that's what it called for at that time.

Gene Dinwiddie was the best tambourine player I ever heard. That guy had a pocket on the tambourine that was deep. You wouldn't need a drummer if you had Dinwiddie play the tambourine: his time was so fierce and his groove was so deep. That's the education that I got with that band: how to play tambourine, where the time should be, how the thing should feel. Butterfield understood that and he would encourage that in people.

I went to audition for Elvin Bishop's band playing bass. Elvin didn't think I was right for his band, but he liked my playing well enough to refer me to go jam with Butterfield at a club called The Generation in New York at 8th Street and Bleecker. After that got torn down, it became Electric Ladyland. I went down there playing bass to jam with Butterfield and I played well enough that he asked me to come audition for guitar. Al Kooper told Butter I could play guitar.

Stained with Tears and Perspiration

The first time I crossed paths with Dylan was on the *New Morning* session. Al Kooper got me on that session. I somehow wound up there.

Dylan was a man of few words. He'd go into the control booth with his guitar, and he'd play and sing the song. However many bars there were or were not there, that was the song: how he played it and sang it.

He would feel stuff sometimes a little odd, like seven-bar phrases and six-beat bars, so we kind of got used to that. We'd just kind of go with it; just react to what he was doing.

Sometimes when you're in the presence of a genius, or a real artist like that, they have something the rest of us don't have. I don't know how to describe it. Dylan was one and Rickie Lee Jones was another. You just feel you're in the presence of true genius.

I don't throw that word "genius" around lightly. Dylan just had this power to draw you in; all the attention in the room went on him. If he didn't say a word and just stood there, everybody was just riveted on him. He just commanded attention.

I considered myself a professional, even at that age. I had the ability to disconnect from any discomfort or personal emotional stuff and just focus on music. Dylan wrote a tune, "Day of the Locusts." The song started with these lyrics: "Oh, the benches were stained with tears and perspiration." Who would come up with a song that started with those lyrics other than Dylan? I was listening to this on headphones while we were playing the song. I remember being really impressed by that.

Voicings

John McLaughlin was my hero because he played so funky and so outside and he was so adventurous. If you look at pictures of John back in 1969, he looked like an accountant. He had a suit and tie. He was coming from that hard-core jazz thing. But he had some other thing going on that was so cool. I tried to cop as much as I could from him, because he knew where to put the time and he knew how to phrase rhythm parts. He was incredibly funky. If you listen to McLaughlin's parts on *Bitches Brew*, his soloing is off the chain. But listen to his rhythm stuff—he's just brilliant.

He took Miles Davis's instructions to heart, Miles said, "Play like you can't play," and McLaughlin got it. He was putting stuff on the offbeat; he was choosing voicings that were really odd. Miles was playing a lot in the Phrygian mode. It's got a flat 2 and a flat 6. That mode is all over *Bitches Brew*. McLaughlin would find those Phrygian flat-2 voicings and pound the shit out of them. He wasn't shy about it: that's what got my attention.

Just be confident, just be all in: that's what McLaughlin is doing when he's putting it on the end of 1. He was making a statement:

a rhythm part is just a melody with notes underneath it. You should play your rhythm parts with the same intensity and confidence and phrasing that you play a single-line part with: a melody or solo.

Albums That Fail

The collapse of the record companies collapsed the underpinnings of artist support. When you take away the artists' support, then what you have is a bunch of very talented people who are ill equipped to wear every hat they have to wear: book keeper, accountant, social media expert, publicist, lawyer. The musician part of it is kind of at the end of the list.

You have to first be a Facebook expert and an Instagram expert. You have to be a videographer and a video editor to be an artist these days. Then after you've done all that, you give the record away because nobody's willing buy records anymore; they can steal them. It's a tough row to hoe as an independent artist these days. Maybe I'm just an old guy that's incredibly stubborn and incredibly unwilling to embrace reality, but I really truly believe that serious artists deserve to be and should be supported as a coldblooded business proposition.

Labels would be better off if they picked a certain number of artists and supported them and let them make three, four, five albums that fail, that don't sell well. Because number five or number six is going to make all their money back times 100. Not only that, it will also be a great piece of art.

The Eagles were f***ing brilliant. That's some of the greatest pop music ever made, and I don't even play that kind of music, but I enjoy the hell out of listening to it. In terms of Steely Dan, *Aja* is a record that could not have been made without the support of the label, and the hundreds and hundreds and hundreds of hours they spent in the studio making that music happen.

As a coldblooded business proposition, those guys are still making money off this Steely Dan name because RCA supported them thirty years ago and let them make *Aja*. They're still cashing in from that investment.

No Yammering

If I mentor somebody, which I currently am, I talk about how a rhythm part is just a melody with notes underneath. There are some basics in music that apply no matter what genre you're in: it's phrasing, it's dynamics. That's what makes music, music. If you're improvising, then that's a whole other separate subject.

It has to do with developing a vocabulary and learning how to split your brain into the listening half and the playing half. To be a good player, you have to first of all be a good listener. That's what Miles Davis understood. Miles was so brilliant at using space. He'd wait till the anticipation was almost unbearable, and then he'd play one note. It would be so perfect a note that everyone would just go "Aahhhhhh."

He understood that music is space and notes, not just notes. The space is more important than the notes. That's why he was so brilliant: because he was such a great listener.

That's what I try to convey to my students: first of all, listen. Don't play until you know what you want to play. Don't just start yammering. The music is about making a statement from your soul to the listener's soul. You're trying to find something in your own soul to express, and express it in such an elegant, efficient way that it will resonate in the listener.

Survival

It may be starting to happen where there are little enclaves of people with resources who want to support art and want to create those bitchin' labels where people can do awesome music and the artists are going to be OK. People with money who care about good music need to pony up. They need to step up to the plate and say, "OK, if I love good music, then I need to support it, because there aren't any labels to do that. I need to create a label or support artists in some way with money."

CHUCK RAINEY

Chuck Rainey grew up in Youngstown, Ohio, as a multi-instrumentalist. After playing the trumpet and baritone horn in high school and college, Rainey picked up the guitar and then bass. He got his professional starts on the road with the saxophonist Sil Austin, later with King Curtis, Roberta Flack, and Aretha Franklin. With King Curtis he shared the bill with The Beatles in the mid-60s on their second tour of the States.

That experience led him into the New York studio scene, where he became firmly ensconced making commercials, jingles, and hit records with Quincy Jones, Merl Saunders, Donny Hathaway, and Steely Dan. He and Bernard Purdie were the preeminent studio rhythm section for musicians of all musics. While providing a deep bottom end, Chuck is a melodic bass player who puts meaning behind every note.

I have interviewed Chuck three times on my radio show: April and July 2013 and August 2017. In these excerpts he discusses knowing your strengths, playing for next to no money to get his name out, the role of a bass player, how to make notes round, and the calling of being a musician.

In the Studio

A lot of people think being a studio musician is easy. Well, it's not that easy. You have to hear things a certain way. There's a certain way that you have to play so it can be produced properly. Like the drummer has to hit the snare in the same place all the time in order to get a consistent sound from the engineer. It takes experience and training to do that. Most road players don't do that. They hit it anywhere, because it's loud and it's amplified.

There's certain things studio musicians come to grips with the more experience they have. So when artists want to do a project, they will go get the musicians they have experience with and who have experience. The same group of people.

Then I'm Ready

When I sit down to play something and nothing is written, because I've listened to a lot of the bass players, I do have an idea of what the bass can do, because I listen to a lot of music.

I think that's one reason I was hired so many times in the past. I always had an idea of what to play, also because I played a lot of other instruments before I played the bass. I want to be consistent in what I'm playing and to make sure that I don't play outside of my strengths as a bass player.

A lot of people play things that they really can't play. I'm old school. Someone tells me what the tempo is, and you get an idea of what the song is, you work at it for about an hour. Then I'm ready.

In recording, if I haven't heard it before, I have too much of a chance to be specific in what I think I want to hear.

Ultimately you end up playing as well as the environment that you're around. My name, after a period of time, became more of a habit. Around 1968 to 73, when you thought of bass in New York and you were doing a recording, you would think of Chuck Rainey or Ron Carter or Richard Davis, because we were always on the scene, playing for nothing sometimes, sometimes playing for little, sometimes playing for union scale. I had a habit of not turning down a gig if I was not already playing or gigging, or because of money.

There's a lot to pay attention to if you're now just coming up. Number one is: you really have to love what you're doing, because this is not an easy business. If you love what you're doing, then a lot of the negative things go over your head, because you love playing. The more you play, the better you get.

Thinking is a large part of what studio musicians have to do. They have to be aware of all the records that are already out, know all the styles, and play a lot. I am a music lover and listen to a lot of music, although I will say luck has a lot to do with it.

A Little Bit More Melodious

I've run across a lot of musicians who emulate what I do. When they get into a situation, they think of me and try and emulate what I did. They don't understand I was playing with certain musicians. My ideas come from listening to the guitar player, or the piano player, and the drummer. I listen to the drummer for feel or for rhythm. Maybe the guitar player or piano player makes a certain indication in the music, just passing by, that gives me an idea to play something a little bit more melodious or just different.

I play more rhythmic than melodious. I'm always thinking rhythm. The bass, for me, is like another drum. It's a drum that's able to voice some kind of melody while I'm playing a rhythm.

Sometimes I played with rhythm sections who weren't really thinking on their feet. Or they were thinking about something other than what the whole group needs to be thinking about. Sometimes alcohol and drugs do get in the way. For a bass player, it was very important to be consistent with what I was doing and let the leader or other instruments build off what I was doing.

A lot of people want to have their own independent voice in the music. They read the press clippings about themselves and they get enamored with the ways they want to be like that. My age group, when we came up, we didn't think about ourselves as individuals. We thought about each other, it was always a team effort.

If the guitar player doesn't like me, I'm not going to get the next gig if the leader asks him who he likes on bass. I want him to like me, so I don't run over anybody. Of course, I haven't always been perfect. I've had to learn all these things I'm talking about the hard way.

Muscles

To make the notes round, you have to hold that neck and just play the notes longer. The upright bass is a much bigger instrument. You get to put your arms around it, and it's a vertical instrument. You'll find that most bass players are very, very strong from the elbow down to their fingertips, because you have to compress the note firmly. And the octaves on the upright bass are about an inch and a half longer from each other than they are on an electric bass, because the neck is so long and so big. You have to have muscle control in your upper arms and your forearms and your hands. However, if you don't play the upright bass, you don't need those kinds of muscles.

By My Doctor

I do this trip with Marlena Shaw every summer to Japan. This year in 2012 it will be our fifth one. The band is a great band; it consists of Harvey Mason, David T. Walker, and Larry Nash. We were the rhythm section on her album *Who Is This Bitch, Anyway?* In Japan it's a very, very popular album. So we go there every summer for 15 or 20 days, doing different performances at different places. Last year, after suffering a stroke, I was told not to go to Japan by my doctor, but Marlena had paid me all up front and I wasn't giving any of the money back. I got myself together the best I could. I suffered a little bit; my hand was a bit stiff; nobody complained. On a lot of the stages, I was unable to do what I wanted to do. It's a family; we all love each other; but physically it was very rough for me. On the encore of the last set on the final night, my hand went totally numb.

I'm a lot stronger now and I'm going to be more comfortable. I think I did OK, but boy was it a struggle, and I haven't struggled in many, many, many, many years.

The Role of the Bass

Back in the day, when I was really playing Top 40 music in order to make a living, and playing on the road with artists who had records, there was always a bass line or a bass part to begin with. The role of the bass is to support the overall music scene at that particular time. That's what the role of the bass is. It's not to solo; it's to keep a consistent rhythmic bass line. Back in the day, you could recognize a song by the bass line; nowadays it's almost impossible.

LEON "NDUGU" CHANCLER

Leon "Ndugu" Chancler was born in Louisiana. But because his father was a successful businessman, the family was driven out of the state by racists. They wound up in Los Angeles, where Ndugu began a career that would culminate in worldwide recognition. His list of credits is staggering: Miles Davis, Weather Report, Harold Land, Eddie Harris, George Duke, Carlos Santana, Michael Jackson. He is most recognized for his drumbeats on Jackson's "Billy Jean." Ndugu left us in 2018, but his spirit and vibrations live on.

I did two radio interviews with Ndugu: in July 2011 and March 2016. I also had an opportunity to interview him in person in July 2017. We talked about following your dream despite the naysayers, how art changes but the concepts don't, a musician's intentions for getting into music to begin with, and playing with Thelonious Monk.

The Business of Creativity

Studio musicians were always paid very well to create and make someone else look good. The only time we did receive something for ourselves was when we wrote something, which is the case for the music business, anyway. If you don't write it, if you don't produce it, you don't get paid. If you just play the session, that's a certain fee. I will say for me, I have been rewarded for most of my work because I was not only the musician but also the businessman, and I always made sure that I got paid. Whatever was due to me, I always made sure that I got it. If there was a royalty due to me, I got it. If there were points due me in any situation, I made sure I got them. There were only a couple of situations where someone beat me, and in order to beat me he had to bankrupt his company. More often than not I got paid.

This is a business. Creativity is creativity. But the business of creativity is the business of creativity. So, you have to always ensure that when you're creating, you're going to be rewarded for your creativity. I don't want to give it away. You know, I never wanted to be one of those musicians who wanted to go down in history as a poor, broke, starving genius. I never wanted to look at it that way. I wanted to be paid for what I did. That's just common business; it's music, but it's business. I always looked at it from the business perspective. I don't think the industry did me an injustice. I don't think I got ripped off. I made enough noise to make sure I got compensated.

Work Your Way Forward

There are a lot of musicians today who are not playing music for the same reasons we did when we started out. We played music in the beginning because we wanted to make a musical statement. There are a lot of people now who don't play music to make a musical statement; they play music to get chicks and fame.

With that, your training is going to be different. Those who have depth, those who have the fundamental training, it is always there. You hear it in their playing, you hear that depth. One of my students asked me, "Why do you like certain young new drummers and you don't like certain other ones?" I said, "Well, I can hear the depth, I can hear the lineage, and I can hear the amount of study that some of the young drummers have done. Who they've paid respect to, who've they've paid homage to, and not just a guy who's assembled a bunch of licks."

There's a difference, because then the music has a connection. A guy used to tell me, "Man, I like the way you solo." I said, "Start with Max Roach and work your way forward."

Music Has Changed, Mentoring Hasn't

When I first got out to LA, there were guys like Earl Palmer, Stix Hooper, Paul Humphrey, Panama Francis, and Shelly Manne. All those guys were established here and doin' it. Harold Land, who was like a mentor to me, and Oliver Nelson and Gerald Wilson, who hired me right out of high school. These guys were great teachers for me, because I got to learn at the foot of the master. And then all the later guys who became my peer group—the Patrice

Rushens, the James Gadsons, the Harvey Masons—we grew into this whole thing together. A lot of us came out of the high school band together and started playin' around together.

Music has changed, but the concept of mentoring and influencing hasn't. I'll find a student who has an interest in playing the music and I will spend time with them and expose them to things, give them guidance, give them advice and listening tools. Sometimes I even feed them and give them equipment. You know mentoring goes a long way, because a lot of times these students don't have the same opportunities; they have the heart but not the opportunities. Mentoring is about helping them find that path, getting on that path, and staying on that path.

Don't Marry it, Just Get Close to it

The thing about Thelonious Monk was, just like a lot of jazz musicians, he didn't use verbal communication a lot of times. Monk never announced what tune he was playing. That's the difference playing with Thelonious and a band nowadays. You had to know the melody of the songs. Monk would just start playing a melody and we would join in. He didn't count things off, he didn't say "We're getting ready to play *Round Midnight*." He would just start playing; you had to know the tune. That made all of us ready for the entire repertoire.

One of the few artists who does that today is Stevie Wonder. He'll just play one of his songs and you have to know it. Most bands rehearse forever, forever, forever, and the tune has one arrangement, one way to do it, and you still may not know the melody but you're studying the groove.

Monk would just start playing the tune and we'd all start playing. You gotta know the key, the melody, the form, and all of that. He played with a whole new arrangement every time. Sometimes Monk would solo first, sometimes someone else would solo first. There were all the musical cues that dictated all of that. That's how the music was made.

I worked with Monk for two weeks straight in San Francisco, and he did not say five words to me the first week. The first week all he'd do was nod his head. That was "hello" for the next few days and that was it. You get used to nonverbal communication. You get used to musical communication, which is one of those dying art forms. The second week we had real conversations off the bandstand. He was opening up to me and we talked about family, we talked about the music, we talked about a whole bunch of things.

Hampton Hawes didn't like to talk much to begin with. His philosophy was really simple: "It's really music. We don't need to talk about it." If we were talking about a musical concept he'd say, "Don't marry it, just get close to it." What that means is, "Let's just play the music and it will play itself." As opposed to, "We're all going to sit here and intellectualize this music and we haven't played a note all day."

If you want to talk about nonverbal communication, his album *High in the Sky* is the album to get. Leroy Vinnegar and Donald Bailey, and they are a live trio. It's seamless, and they go through all of these tunes without any type of verbal communication.

Music Is a Meal

By the late 70s/early 80s radio started to become compartmentalized and they started naming directions in music: in jazz, in all the different styles of music. That channeled the listener to think that if it didn't fall under this umbrella or that umbrella it wasn't that kind of music. And at that point, jazz had already grown to be so many different things that you couldn't just capsulize it and say it was A, B, C, or D. It was all of the above.

The station would say "We're a traditional jazz station; we only play A, B, and C." OK, so if that's all you play, then what's to say that this is or isn't jazz? So if you have an artist who has gone so far away from jazz, we don't know if that fits. Really? Well, how far did they go away from jazz? My biggest beef with that is that Miles Davis was always Miles Davis. Now it might not have been the

Miles Davis you grew up on, might not have been the Miles Davis that you liked, but he was always Miles Davis—a jazz musician. Yes, the sound changed; yes, the instrumentation changed; but he was still playing like Miles. People start to lose sight of the inner concept of diversity.

Music *is* like a meal. You don't just eat beef for a meal. You have all these things that round out a good meal. So you look at music the same way: you don't want everything on your plate to be the same. You want your plate to have some diversity, and that's what the music does. But you can't do that if you believe that everything is based on this one concept or sound. That takes the global diversity appeal away from you, and it says that your own self is compartmentalized.

Your Dream Is on You
A lot of people don't have the stick-to-it-iveness or the belief and faith in themselves to pursue their dream. They look at the dream as just a dream that could never become reality. Some of them are fed misinformation about it being a reality and others aren't.

If you're following your dream, you're following *your* dream. That has nothing to do with what everyone else feels about what your dream is, how to follow it, or anything else. That yearning and urge inside of you to follow your dream starts with you. It ends with you. The success of you following your dream is on you.

The crossroads are relationships and family: that's a major hurdle in artists following their dream. How do you balance having a family, and going out and playing the music and being dedicated to playing the music? It's easier when you can sustain yourself and help your environment, your environment being your family. If you can have a family, and work, and do music, then it's an unselfish approach to being a family person. If you can't, then on both sides you're selfishly shortchanging one side or the other.

You have to have people around you who believe in you and your vision and your dream. If those people don't believe in you and your dream, they're going to be draining you anyway. In that dream, that's going to take a lot away from you and it's going to take a lot away from your relationship. At some point something has to give.

There has to be a certain amount of faith and belief in a person from the beginning. In my early years, I had to make sure that whomever I was dealing with understood my plight as an artist, but also understood my goals as an artist and my responsibilities to my family as an artist.

You always pull from positive, and if you always pull from positive the negative will never really have a chance to fester and grow enough for you to have any doubt. The first thing that happens to you from really pursuing what you really believe in is the doubt that it may not work. Well, you'll never know if it works until you try it. If you never try it, you never know. There are so many people who say, "Man, if only I had stuck to playing music, I would be blah, blah, blah...." How can you do that if you're doubting what you're doing in the first place?

EMIL RICHARDS

Emil Richards was born in Hartford, Connecticut in 1932. His musical career started at 13, playing xylophone with Arthur Fielder and the Boston Pops. He is a trailblazer of new music in the West. He's a microtonal master, a musician who gets off messing with the traditional Western twelve-tone scale and breaking it into microtones. He was the assistant band leader of the first Calvary Army Band in Japan in the early 1950s, saw the reconstruction of that country, and lent a hand in healing it through music. He has worked on countless film scores with cats such as Jerry Goldsmith, John Williams, and Henry Mancini. He toured the world with Frank Sinatra, was part of Frank Zappa's Abnuceals Emuukha Electric Orchestra, and toured for years with George Shearing, Count Basie, and George Harrison. He discovered Transcendental Meditation with Maharishi Mahesh Yogi, which helped him find peace and salvation. He has over 760 percussion instruments in his collection.

I first connected with Emil telephonically on my radio show in May 2011, then at his home in Toluca Lake, CA in June 2012, and Facebook Lives in December 2017 and November 2018.

A Life of Rhythm

I am a percussion freak. I have ended up with the most percussion instruments in the United States.

Strings, brass, woodwinds—percussion is always at the bottom. It's always at the bottom with the guy who's carrying the freakin' music.

Do the Math

I can't improvise without thinking of mathematics. I don't compose a song without thinking of mathematics. It is so essential to rhythm and to music. I go to different colleges all across the country, and the world, giving clinics on odd time rhythms, Indian rhythms, as they relate to our 4/4 jazz playing.

It not only helps with your improvisation, but it helps with composition, reading skills. It's an additive to what you already know musically. I have such joy going to different colleges and teaching this. I intend to do this for the rest of my days. When you see the kids' faces and they realize what they're doing, it's amazing.

"You're Corny"

My mother was the first person in Connecticut with a liquor license. My father and mother never drank, but there was always liquor in the house. I started drinking at 8 years old. I grew up in an all-black neighborhood, so I got turned on to pot at 10 years old. I was doing all of that real early. When cocaine came on the scene, I was doing that real early.

I was lucky enough to meet Tommy Mace who said, "Heroin is a no-no. Anybody who tells you you're corny, you tell them they're corny for trying to turn you on to something like that." I was very grateful to this guy (and lucky), who took me through those years.

A Lot of Xylophone

My dad ran away from home at 15 and stowed away on a ship. He landed in Quebec, Canada and walked across the border. His oldest brother was living in Hartford, Connecticut. My mother was 3 years old when she came over with her parents. My grandfather Emilio was a flute player with the symphony in Sicily. He came to America and couldn't get a job as a musician, so he became a barber at the Navy Base in New London, Connecticut.

My folks met at an early age. My dad was 26 and my mom was 17 when they got married. My brother and I showed up a few years later.

I got into music when I was six years old. My folks both loved opera. We got to hear a lot of Italian folk music and all the opera from the leading composers in Italy.

When I was in 10th grade, Arthur Fiedler came to town to do six concerts with the Boston Pops. After the first rehearsal, he told the head of the percussion department, "I need somebody who can really play a lot of xylophone." I got called in and not only did those six concerts, but I stayed with the orchestra until I got drafted at 22 years old.

My First Earthquake

I didn't want to join the army, I wanted to get drafted. If you joined it was three years, if you got drafted it was two years. I lucked out and got into a band in Japan.

We landed in Sendai, that's where my base was. No one had heard of Sendai, before the terrible earthquake and tsunami. My first night in Sendai I thought someone had picked me up and thrown me on the floor. Coming from the East Coast, that was my first earthquake in 1954.

We were there to improve our relations with Japan. The war had only been over for ten years. It was still fresh in the Japanese people's minds that we were the bad guys. We hooked up with a Japanese Army band. We traveled up and down the country bettering relations, showing that both army bands could work together and play together. We did concerts going up and down the country.

My first furlough was a fifteen-day leave from Sendai and I went to Tokyo. I heard what I thought was a record of Bud Powell playing piano. I went downstairs to this club and here's this young woman, Toshiko Akiyoshi, playing all of Bud Powell's music. There was a vibraphone on the stage, so I just jumped up and started playing with her. The alto saxophonist was Sadeo Watanabe and he played just like Charlie Parker. I was in heaven. I met people playing all the jazz I had grown up with. They were so appreciative of American jazz and could really play it. Sadeo did a whole series of films for Japan showing the roots of how jazz in the U.S.

When I got back from Japan I went to New York, because I thought I would want to start doing some studio work in New York. I lasted a short time playing around New York with Charles Mingus, Flip Phillips, Ed Shaughnessy, and Ed Thigpen. I got an audition for the George Shearing Quintet. I wasn't in New York a year before I was back out on the road for almost four years with the George Shearing Quintet traveling across the U.S. One year we did it nine times back and forth by car. That was a great experience, with Al McKibbon and Armando Peraza.

My first day in LA, I was working in the studios. I had met Paul Horn on the road; he was with Chico Hamilton when I was with George Shearing. He had a working quartet, so the first day I arrived we formed a quintet. We were playing on the Sunset Strip at Club Renaissance. I recorded in the studio with Paul and met Nelson Riddle; and through him I started to do some live shows with Frank Sinatra.

My first trip to India was with Sinatra. It so fascinated me that when I started meditating, I said, "How do they know to give a person a mantra? How do you meditate on a mantra?" I had to go to India and study deeper about meditation. Maharishi didn't approach it from a spiritual point of view, although you seem to become more spiritual with the practice of meditation. Maharishi had a doctoral degree in science. He approached from a very scientific point of view. It's amazing how such a simple technique could get you to go within yourself and bring out so much good and quality of life.

Filled the Belly
We were all working towards getting John F. Kennedy elected president and we did a commercial called "High Hopes." We had "high hopes" for Jack Kennedy to become president.

As soon as he became president, he asked Frank Sinatra if he would do a world tour for underprivileged children and found hospitals wherever we went. Well, Frank said, "I'll do you one better. I'll pay for the trip myself. I have my own jet. You tell me what countries you want us to go to, and we'll go." Kennedy said, "Then we'll have the ambassador of each country meet you and get you through customs."

That tour was really when I started to collect instruments. We didn't have to worry about customs, so I filled the belly of Frank's plane with ethnic percussive instruments from around the world. We went to Israel for ten days and founded a hospital which, at that time, was on the Israeli/Palestinian border.

Judge Your Day

In 1962, I was 30 years old and so many great things happened to me. I got into Transcendental Meditation and I met a lot of the Indian musicians. I had been studying with someone who was a student of Ravi Shankar. As a result, I met Ravi Shankar and started to go to India a lot, to not only study mediation but study music, and to play with Ravi Shankar and all his musicians.

I wound up in a little hut in the side of the Himalayas. Every evening Maharishi would give talks that really imparted some great knowledge to everybody. I went with the second group. The Beatles had just left; they were the first group to see Maharishi.

During the first round of meditating, Maharishi made the people (Donovan, Paul Horn, The Beatles, Mia Farrow) meditate for long periods of time—all day every day. The people who were in that first group freaked out, because they had been taking a lot of LSD prior to leaving for India. Their nervous systems couldn't really take it. Maharishi didn't realize how badly they had been messed up with drugs.

The second course was right after that, and he made us meditate all day long, but he let us break every hour for ten or fifteen minutes to come out, go to the cafeteria, and have some vegetarian food. We'd take a break and then go back in to meditate again. He changed this on the second cycle, which I was fortunate enough to be a part of.

People would come to the lectures at night with Maharishi and they'd say, "Maharishi, this is what happened during my meditation, this is what happened after I started meditating."

Maharishi used to say, "Don't judge your meditation, just judge your living. See what's happening with your life, if anything has changed or improved. Don't judge the meditation, judge your day."

It's everything you think you're getting with drugs, but the drugs weren't lasting. It took me a while; I didn't stop right away. Being a musician, I still messed up quite a bit. Eventually I could get to all those states, and then some, through meditation.

The first retreat we went on, we met Maharishi in Squaw Valley. Paul Horn and I rented a house with Robby Krieger and John Densmore of The Doors. We were there for long meditations and for learning more about meditation. It just so happened we really got together with music and became part of the beginning structure of learning all about Indian rhythms and microtonal music and continuing all our studies with both meditation and music. To this day I'm still very close to Robby and John. I don't see them as much as I used to, but when I do see them it's like we've never been apart. We know all of that good feeling is still there.

Their Lips Are Dead

I played a lot of cartoon music, and that is the hardest music to play. Fred Flintstone falling down the stairs (playing frenetically) is written out. It enhanced my sight-reading enormously to play cartoons. The xylophone, which is like a marimba only starting up higher, had a comedic sound to it. Consequently, it was used a lot in cartoon music.

What I do on a movie call is, I get a call, "You're going to do four days at Warner Brothers with John Williams working on *E.T.*"

If it's a Warner Brothers picture. I call over and get ahold of the orchestrator and the copyist. About four days before the movie I say, "What's the list of percussive instruments that I'm going to need for this picture?"

They tell me that five percussionists will be needed for the session. Here's a list of all the instruments that you're going to need for the gig. We call the cartage company, where all my stuff is stored. They send the instruments to the studio on the day we're supposed to be there. Everything that we need to play for four days we set up: mallet instruments, vibes, marimbas, bells, chimes. We uncover them and then open the trunks and take out triangles, wood blocks, tom-toms, anything else we're going to need.

When I first got to town, I did all "this," because none of this was happening.

I would instruct the copyist, on the very first page of our music—which was sometimes 7 to 12 to 15 pages long—to put all five parts on our piece of music, so that we could see what everybody was playing. You got a lot of pages when you got five lines going; you can only put two lines of music and you've got to keep going, page after page. The very first page I would tell the copyist, "You write every percussion instrument that we're supposed to play on that beginning page, so we don't come to any surprises on page 17. We know all the instruments that we're going to need."

You cannot record every day of your life and jive. There have been times when the French horns and brass, their lips are dead, and the conductor would say, "Oh, man, we finally got a good one, thanks for doing one more." I'd say, "Sorry, I f***** up, we've got to do it again." They'd want to kill me, but you know what? When they leave the studio, and the brass guy goes back to listen to it and he hears my mistakes that cannot be corrected, I would never be working in this town. The playback is a mirror that hits you in the face and does not tell a lie. Today with Pro Tools, you can fix all that stuff.

Separate Double

The first double scale was 50% and any double after that was 20%. We only had two doubles when I first got here to LA, traps and mallets.

From Shelly Manne to Irv Cottler to Milt Holland to Alvin Stoller on down, we got every drummer in town, every mallet player, and we decided what was going to be a double. We gave the Union a list of twenty-five different percussion instruments. It was more than enough.

We had one list of Latin instruments (bongos/congas), another list of percussion instruments. Anything that was not on that list we construed as a separate double, like steel drums. It takes a lifetime to learn steel drums, tabla drums. None of us were really good tabla players, because tabla players spend a lifetime learning their instrument. The unions wouldn't hire a tabla player; they wanted the percussionist to be able to play all those instruments. Every drummer in town met at my house two Sundays a month for close to a year to build these lists.

We felt it only fair we get compensated we thought we deserved for the doubles. It took a long time, a lot of meetings, and when we presented it to management, they had no complaints with it, because we were being fair, for sure. Not only did we have to learn to play these instruments, we had to buy them.

When you're playing the kind of music that you play in the studios, you're reading new music that you never saw before, and they want to record it. Being able to record it, you have to be such a great sight-reader to play it down the first time cold. That kind of wears on your psyche. You need a break, like anyone else's psyche.

He Wasn't Afraid

Ravi Shankar introduced me to George Harrison. We became fast friends. I was crocheting hats, and when we went on tour, I crocheted hats and scarves for everybody in the band. The band consisted of Indian musicians and American musicians: Chuck Findley, Tom Scott, Willie Weeks, Andy Newmark, Billy Preston, Robben Ford.

We did two shows each night. Ravi came out first with all the Indian guys along with me, Tom Scott, and Robben Ford, and we'd do a whole set of Indian music. Then they'd leave the stage and we would do the jazz set.

I loved George Harrison. He may not have been the best guitar player in the world, but his love of music and his unembarrassed attitude towards music were infectious. He was around a lot of good musicians on that tour, and he didn't care who heard him play, he just played. He wanted to play all the time. He wasn't embarrassed to play anything in front of everybody. He was there to also learn. He was more than just "a Beatle." He was a humble player, and he impressed the hell out of me. He wasn't afraid to play with all the heavy cats. The one thing that impressed me the most about him was, he was never without his guitar.

Alla Rakha had a private plane that we traveled in all over the US. Allah was my "plane-seat buddy." I had all the barf bags from the airplane and I was writing down all the rhythms that Alla would recite. I would say, "Alla, just do that one again, I didn't quite catch the end part."

Chuck Findley's asleep behind us and he says, "I got that one, just have him go on." Chuck was a trumpet player, and not a percussionist, but everything Alla did, he had down, without even writing it down. Alla kept waking him up with all the fantastic things he was saying.

What Do You Want?

I knew Jim Keltner for a long time and never knew he played jazz until I went out to hear him play with some guys and freaked out.

In all the years we hung out together my closest experience with Jim came when we were with George Harrison. George asked Jim to come on tour with us and Jim said, "I'm sorry, George, I've just been on the road too much. My kids are young, they're missing their dad, and my wife would like me to stay home too." George said, "Let's take the kids on the road. We'll get a private tutor." Keltner said, "I never seem to come out ahead moneywise when I go on tour." George said, "I won't give you money, I'll buy you a car. What do you want? I just want you with us."

I didn't know any of that at the time, but Jim showed up on the tour. His children came every once in a while, and his wife. That's how we really got tight.

See also Emil Richards with Tom Di Nardo, *Wonderful World of Percussion: My Life Behind Bars* (BearManor Media, 2013).

DAVID SPINOZZA

David Spinozza is a New York based guitarist and producer. His studio acumen is evident on Paul McCartney's *Ram* album, Yoko Ono's *Feeling the Space*, and John Lennon's *Mind Games*. He's played on countless hit records, such as Don McLean's *American Pie*, B. B. King *In London*, and Dr. John's *In the Right Place*.

Included in these excerpts is David's account of a taxi driver who thought he was full of it when one of his solos came on the radio, the blending of all musics that was occurring, how open the musicians were to these influences, how the function of music has changed in our society, and how music that is recorded today isn't always worthy of being recorded.

Demanding or Commanding

I like leaders that don't get rattled. A lot of times you see leaders and they think they have to lead with an iron fist and make everybody uptight. I think that works against musicians to do that. Even in the classical world there are conductors who think you have to stay on the orchestra to keep them playing, and they run an orchestra like it's an army. I like leaders that have their shit together. They're not fearful themselves, so they don't make the band fearful. I think musicians play better when they're not afraid. Arif Mardin is a good example; so is Quincy Jones. Not only was Arif a good musician, producer, and arranger, but he had that ability to make you want to play for him. That's a great quality in a leader. It's the difference between demanding your attention and commanding it.

All Fall Down

At the time I was working with Carly Simon, she introduced me to James Taylor. I was her musical director for about three years. That band, L'image, had Mike Mainieri. Steve Gadd was in it, Tony Levin. We were backing Carly, and I had just done my record for A&M records.

We would open up for her, and then she would come out and do her set. She had just started to date James and he wanted to do another record. One of the songs, "Let It All Fall Down," was about Richard Nixon resigning. Apparently, James had tried to record it before, but didn't like the way it came out. He was liking my work with Carly and he said to me, "There's this song, if you can make it sound good in the studio, you can produce my next record." I was like, "What?!" He was already big at that point. I brought the band in, he liked the way it came out and said, "Well, let me play you the rest of the songs; you are going to produce my next record."

Watch Out for This Guy

After about the first four or five years of playing sessions I was pretty confident. There was always one little fear for me. When you start playing dates there were not a lot of rehearsals, you had to come in and sight-read stuff, and my reading wasn't as good as my ears, so I was always studying to stay ahead of it. I kept worrying about that one session where somebody was going to come in, put a guitar part in front of me that I couldn't play, and I'd have to say, "Sorry I can't do this." I'd have to remove myself from the session. That fear was always there.

Reading on a guitar can be kind of iffy. It's not like reading on a horn, when you read one note at a time. There's so many different ways to do something on the guitar. There were a few sessions where I sweated through the guitar part. I couldn't immediately read it. I had to shed it for a minute and figure it out.

You got to see the same cats. Day in and day out, I would see the same 50 musicians. I'd see the Brecker Brothers, I'd see Steve Gadd, I'd see Rick Marotta, I'd see Mike Mainieri. At one time I was doing 15 recording sessions a week. It could be Aretha Franklin in the morning and Les McCann in the evening. The next day it could be Roberta Flack and then a jingle. After a while it became like a family of musicians that were doing a lot of this work in NYC.

I was so young when I got called for dates. I didn't even know who Eric Gale was. I remember playing on some RnB dates, and Bernard Purdie would be playing drums and Chuck Rainey on bass. Either Richard Tee or Paul Griffin on piano. They'd joke around saying, "Hey, Eric, watch out for this guy, David Spinozza."

Music in Society

If we could all agree on words, then lawyers wouldn't be arguing with each other. If everything meant something exactly, and you could express the truth perfectly and everybody got it the same, that would make life easy. Unfortunately, it's not like that. We have all the code words. "Jazz." What's "hip hop," really? It's just a term. People say, "Oh, that's Southern country rock." What is that?

People's patience, people's attention spans, have changed. And the function of music in society has changed. It's never something to focus on now. When "smooth jazz" came out, people would say, "Oh, this is great music to talk over." I thought, "Wow, when I was growing up, we didn't talk over music." If you put an album on, you listened from beginning to end.

Why has the function of music as the focus changed? I don't know why. If I did, I could sell millions of recordings.

Oh, That's Me

I only played the guitar solo on the song "Right Place, Wrong Time." The Meters were the rhythm section on that album. I've done a lot of sessions with Dr. John. I never knew him as that; I always knew him as Mac. I was at Atlantic Records one day, coming out of a session. I was waiting for the elevator, and Dr. John and Arif Mardin come out of the mix room. They were already mixing that record and apparently they forgot to put a solo on that song. If I'm not mistaken, it was going to be a sax solo.

They said, "Spinozza, you got a minute? Could you come in and throw a solo on this song?" I was on my way to a jingle date. I was mostly doing commercials, and even the recording scene was changing. I said, "I got twenty minutes." They said, "You'll hear it, you'll hear it. Come on." I go into this little mix room and there was a little Fender amp in there. I plugged it in and they threw a mic on it. They teed it up right to where the solo was. I never heard the whole song. They said, "It's in the key of E flat; play something bluesy." I took my guitar out and I remember my G string was out of tune. I put the headphones on and played the solo

To this day it's hard for me to listen to that solo, because one of the notes I overbent to some note I wasn't trying to bend it to, because I thought the string was out of tune. So I tuned up and said, "Okay let me try one more." They said, "No, that's it. It's magic; you're done." I remember leaving the studio kind of dejected because I thought I could have played something better than that.

Cut to NYC two or three months later, I'm in a yellow cab and I got three guitars hanging off me. That song comes on the radio, but I don't recognize it because I've never heard it. It gets to the solo, and the cab driver turns around and says, "You'll appreciate this. You're a guitar player. This is my new favorite guitar solo," and he turns it up. I recognize that it's me and in a knee-jerk reaction say, "Oh, that's me." He goes, "Yea, right, buddy," and he turns it off because he thinks I'm full of sh*t.

PART 2

IN MEMORIAM NEAL CASAL

I intended from the beginning to include Neal Casal in this book, partly because I wanted to have one of my peers. In July 2019, I methodically went through the transcripts of the two radio interviews I did with him and sent them along to him. I also sent him a waiver release to sign, giving me permission to use the content. The following is our communication via text:

Jake: Hey, man. Can you read the excerpts, sign that waiver release, and get it back to me by Wednesday? Looking to get this book out asap. See you on CATS tour.

Neal: Sorry for delay, man. Spaced. Do I have to print it and mail it to you? Psyched. man.

Neal: Waiver sent via mail (snail).

Jake: Thanks, my man.

Less than two weeks after these texts, Neal tragically took his own life. There is no reason that can explain why someone as talented and classy as Neal would do something like that. It is a jolting reminder that we are all dealing with our own madness, trying to stay comfortable in our own skin, and balancing being a giver and receiver of others' energy on a regular basis.

I had the opportunity to see Neal play live over a dozen times in several different contexts and spend time with him off the bandstand. I didn't know Neal as well as others, but we were getting closer and he was a focal point for my exploration as a music journalist. He worked hard, he had an eclectic and wide palette when it came to music, he wore his emotions on his sleeve, he kept improving, he had high expectations for himself, and he was a candid and honest human being. These are all traits that I would like to accentuate to my generation and future generations of artists.

I went out to dinner with Neal before a gig with the Chris Robinson Brotherhood in Riverhead, New York in June 2019. He said, "Jake, you're a stone soul groover." Neal understood my pocket as an avid fan of sound and sonic expansion. It was a mutual admiration society.

Celebrate Neal Casal and channel his spirit to affect positive change in your world. As the great Ken Kesey said, "Spirit is the only currency."

As he would always sign off his texts to me, "Sail on, Sayla."

The singer-songwriter **NEAL CASAL** was born in New Jersey. He was inspired early in his life by the messages in songs from bands across the entire musical spectrum. He did not go to the academy and he did not learn facility and chops first. He learned music by ear and always had a unique ability to serve the song. Maybe that involves creating a little bridge to complete a tune. Maybe that involves playing a solo that fits the mood of a particular composition. Maybe it's playing his favorite role of second-in-command, backing up the leader and inspiring his band-mates to be themselves. Throughout his career he found himself in all types of musical situations and melded those experiences together in a way that enhanced his musicianship and fearlessness on the bandstand. He committed suicide in August 2019.

I did two radio interviews with Neal on my radio show: in July 2016 and June 2017. We talked about: the calling of a musician, the genesis of his interest in songwriting, how he found his way into the world of The Grateful Dead and Chris Robinson, what the qualities of effective leadership are, and how he learned to not scheme or think about the future but, rather, sweeten the distance and ride the wave of now.

Get to the Gold
Sometimes we all need to be reminded to let the music be the guide. I get out of the way when the music's good, and get in the way when it's bad. I try not to worry so much about these things.

As Chris Robinson says, "Follow the muse and it will take care of you." He's right about that. If you keep yourself in the right place, you keep yourself following the right idea, you may muddle through the weeds for a while, but you pay your dues and you will be rewarded. I've learned to hang in there and persevere, and things work out. If you quit and you give up too soon, you won't get to the gold.

A Lifetime That People Don't Know

My first solo record came out in 1995. I made a lot of them, a lot of songs, where it's just me singing songs that I wrote and put bands together to listen to. I toured all through Europe and the States: that's what I did.

My friend John Ginty was my cohort back then, and we learned the ropes together. I was a leader and I've done this for a long time. It's a lifetime that people don't know about me. There was a whole other thing that happened before Ryan Adams, before any of this Jam Circuit.

It was all based on songwriting. I was a little bit a part of the *No Depression* scene and The Jayhawks and Uncle Tupelo and Joe Henry: that's where I lived. That's what I was into. I wasn't so much into the jam scene, although I played The Wetlands, but that's not where I resided. I spent years learning how to write songs and make records. How to record was a big thing for me. There was a whole other career for me, before Ryan, and before the Chris Robinson Brotherhood. All of that knowledge and work I put in is what built the foundation to make me the musician I am now. That's why I've been able to thrive, somewhat, in this world. I'm not the virtuosic guitar player that a lot of my friends are, but I have a lot of other skills and I bring a lot to the table, because of the work I've put in in so many areas for decades.

Shoved out the Door

The one thing I am very fortunate to have is a true passion for music. Meaning, the reasons that I play music and the reason I made a life in music were authentic ones.

I've been able to get through times of adversity because of the reasons why I do it in the first place. It's real to me, you know. It was never about making money; it wasn't to get anywhere. There was no agenda other than to really be involved in the music for the sake of the music.

A lot of times when you get shaken to your core, if you're not into something for the right reasons you'll end up getting out of it.

You'll be taken out of it, if your truth isn't very sound.

I'm not the best musician in the world. I'm struggling for everything I can get. I've been through several times when I was down and out ready to be shoved out the door. I've been allowed to stay in this because the reasons that I do it are real. That's really the chief thing I have going for me. It brings a tear to the eye.

Not that I'm Desperate

As a kid I was drawn to music because there was something in me that wanted to get out of where I was. Playing the guitar and singing were the only things that were going to get me out of my little town. There's nothing really wrong with my little town where I come from. But in my dramatic young mind, the idea of a mundane life—what I saw as a dead-end kind of life—I had to get out. There was only one way for me to do that and that was by playing music and singing. There was and remains a certain desperation there. Not that I'm desperate for anything, but there is a pleading, there is a needing to do it, that I can't fully explain.

A Matter of Life and Death

When I first left home I was living in Ann Arbor, Michigan, I was playing in this band, and I lived in a barn. I had absolutely no money. I was stealing food from a gas station: ramen noodles and cans of soup, the time-honored tradition of starving musicians. I lived very close to the campus. Every day I would walk around that campus because there were a lot of shops and restaurants and record stores.

I would be walking side by side, almost arm and arm with kids that were my exact same age. They were all going to college and I wasn't. I was living in a freezing barn and starving and stealing food, just so I could play guitar in a rock and roll band. Never once did it occur to me that I should be doing what the students were doing. I never ever doubted myself and I never thought, "Well, maybe I should go to college like they are. because it's a smarter move." It never dawned on me until at least 15 years later that

that's how badly I wanted to do "this." That's how much it meant to me, and it really was a matter of life or death back then.

What Songs Can Do for us
My need to write songs started from day one of hearing music. You hear something as tried and true as "Ramblin' Man" by the Allman Brothers and hear what an absolutely great song that is on every level. The composition is the whole thing.

Even silly songs like Carpenters' songs, when you really get down to them, are really pieces of work and writing. As I got into my songwriting life, I discovered Townes Van Zandt, Guy Clark, Jackson Browne's early records—the list is extremely long.

I got fascinated with it because songs move me, stories move me, lyrics move me. The mythology of songs lit my imagination on fire. I heard "Sympathy for the Devil" by The Rolling Stones when I was 9 years old, and those lyrics fascinated me to no end. They opened the door to politics for me, to war, to social issues. It's endless what songs can do for us. I'm in the business of making songs, playing songs. I've written a few myself. That's where Chris Robinson and I actually find a lot of common ground. You've got to have a song to sing at the end of the day. You've got to be able to sing that song, too. He and I are sticklers for that.

I've made many records under my own name. I've written a lot of songs, and a few I consider great songs. The rest of them are pretty good, and then there are some clunkers rattling around in the can.

Songwriting is constantly gnawing at me. The idea of writing songs, and the need to write what I feel are good songs, gnaws at me stronger than almost anything else in life. I thought about "Does the idea of having a family gnaw at me as hard as this?" No, it doesn't.

The Chase Is on
Every path of music, everything that we're after—lyrics, songwriting, singing—there's no complacency ever. There isn't any

part of my creative life that I feel satisfied with. I've done some good work, and some work that I'm really proud of—that I would give to anyone and put up against most things and say, "Hey, that's great."

I've done a lot of good work, but as far as being satisfied with my level of ability, and what I'm doing—no, not even close. As a matter of fact, the farther I go into this, the more there is to learn, and the chase is on. Once you really know what's out there, you realize it's an endless well.

It's like studying space: "Wait, we thought that was the end, but somebody made a new telescope that can see way further. So where we thought it ended before, it absolutely doesn't. We have no idea, and the whole thing is way bigger than we ever thought." So forget about thinking you know everything, 'cause you don't. That's why I love being in this music so much, because of its infinite nature.

This Little Dream I Was Having

I had a record deal when I was a solo artist another lifetime ago. The deal was for a couple of years, and I made this record on a major label back in the 1990s. The record came out and I had high hopes for it, and I was trying really hard, but nothing really happened.

It was only a few months after the record came out that I was on tour with my band in Nashville and I called my manager, Gary Waldman, from the road to see how things were going. He informed me, right before I was about to go on stage, that I had been dropped by the label.

Everything went away at that point, and whatever money I was living on was gone. Every little bit of support I had was gone. And that little dream I was having got crushed. Right there, that's a point where I've seen a lot of people not make it through that.

I didn't know what I was going to do, I didn't really have anything going on. I hung in through the adversity and kept writing songs. I resolved to make another record quickly after that on a much smaller budget, and I did it and somehow found my way.

That's a very typical story for an artist at that time. For the 1990s that was a very typical story: it happened every five minutes. Some little song writer got a little deal, and they were all excited about it, and they were allowed to make a record, and when something didn't happen with it, they got dropped.

I had support from Gary Waldman, who I still work with to this day. He always stuck by me. It was still up to me to find out what I was going to do. I had to find the creativity to come up with more songs to keep myself going.

Chris Robinson saw more in me than I could. I appreciate him for that, I really do. I took him up on his challenge. He said, "Look, you're going to do this. I need a guitar player. I need somebody to do it. It might as well be you."

I replied, "You're absolutely right. What better do I have to do than better myself as a musician? If you look at Chris, he's a savvy guy and he's been surrounded by great musicians his entire career. He's had a lot of great guitar players. He knows a good one when he hears one.

Another thing about Chris is that he's brave. I've learned a lot from him on that. Go and get out in front of people with a song that he just wrote, that no one's ever heard before—that's not an easy thing to do, man. He is not afraid to put himself out there and fail and pick himself up and dust himself off and then rise to great heights. The guy goes for it. Every time Chris gets up on stage, he goes for it. I've never seen him phone in a performance ever, and I've done hundreds and hundreds of gigs with him at this point and we've been in some adverse situations. We've played some crappy places after several nights of little sleep. Touring is hard; it can be hard. That dude—when it comes to music and how he approaches it—is the real thing. It's easy for me to support him, because I believe in the cat. When it comes down to opening your mouth to sing and stepping up to the plate—he's there. How else would I approach it? I've got to be there, too.

You're the Cat!

Chris Robinson has inspired me deeply at two different points in my life. In the early 90s, I was a big fan of The Black Crowes. The preaching that he did back then was just as relevant as it is now. He was telling people to "Wake up, man, and get yourself into some really good music. Look past what you're being shown at level one. You have to go many, many levels down to really get to the substance. Then you can check in with yourself and see how you're doing at that point." He was saying that stuff from day one of his career and he's still living it now.

I wasn't really comfortable being one of those "guitar guitar" guys when I joined CRB. Chris said, "You're going to be the lead guy and you're going to play these really long instrumental things. You're the cat!"

I was like, "No, I've never been that cat. That's not me, I love YES, and I love The Grateful Dead, but I've never been a lead guitar improviser." I was always into shorter song forms. I had never played that expansively before and I was afraid of getting out into this jam world with all these virtuoso musicians, which I don't consider myself to be.

I got into it, and here I am doing my best, slugging it out with all the pros. I do enjoy expanding a lot and I got a pretty good sense of humor, so I can just kind of deal with it. It's all in the wind at the end of the day.

Chris doesn't tell anyone what to play. There's a theory for the band and it's based on psychedelic music. We're all jazz heads. Not that we can really play that way, but we base our instrumental ideas and openness on the records that we love. There's really no restriction. Everybody polices themselves as far as what they play and what they bring to it.

Upstarts Like Me

My friendship with Phil Lesh came along through the Chris Robinson Brotherhood. He sat in with us several times.

I had known Phil beforehand when I played with Ryan Adams

& The Cardinals. Phil was a big Ryan fan and sat in with that band a couple of times, so I knew him a little bit. Then I met him again with the CRB, and some nice things fell together when Phil opened for our big Terrapin Crossroads date. He needed musicians to fill out his roster with the many shows that were going on there. I was lucky enough to be standing in the right place when he needed me. He remembered me and started inviting me up to play with him. That's where my education in the jam band world really started. I didn't know the music. I knew the songs, but I didn't know how to play them, because when I was younger, I was working on my own songs. I was never a cover guy, ever. I had to catch up on all that music very quickly and I worked my ass off to at least get a handle on the Grateful Dead catalog.

Now I have the ability to play with one of the grandmasters and creators of this entire world, who still happens to be one of the greatest musicians in the world. He's willing to play with upstarts like me and show me the ropes. I took that very, very seriously.

Why Stay Where You Are?

My life as a musician has expanded. I got excited about trying to break through my own boundaries into places where I'm not comfortable. Playing with Phil very much does that for me. Particularly in the beginning, it pushed me way out of my comfort zone, and I found myself standing next to Jimmy Herring and I found myself standing next to Warren Haynes, I found myself next to Stanley Jordan, I get to play with Joe Russo. Adam MacDougall blows my mind on a daily basis. It's a caliber of people I just wasn't around before. I had to raise my game, and in doing that I got better. Why stay where you are? I learned plenty where I was before; why not give this a shot? Hard Working Americans called and said, "Come play." Phil called and said, "Come play." I was not prepared for that. I had to learn really quickly, and suddenly I get the call to make the music for the Fare Thee Well shows.

I love being a part of this world. I'm rather new to it. I enjoy it. I don't find it limiting, yet. And if there's another place where this music can exist or we can expand it, that's great. I think the music will tell us; the world will tell us. But I'm not going to try and force myself into any other situation. I'm certainly not going to go knocking on anyone's door to be heard. I'm not going to try and appeal to any younger hipster people, or anything like that.

I'm just going to appreciate exactly where I'm at. I'm going to keep on playing music that's interesting to me, and it will find its way. I'm not trying to get rid of the responsibility of having to answer that question. But every time I've overthought it and place myself somewhere, it always falls flat. Whenever I kind of just let it go and follow my instincts and go for it, that's when the best things happen. That's why Circles happened.

Fare Thee Well

Justin Kreutzmann ended up doing the visuals for the Fare Thee Well shows. He asked me if I would make all the music for those shows. That was mind-blowing and worked out really well. Justin is a brother I'm indebted to for sure.

He told me there were going to be big screens on each side of the stage at these shows. He was putting together visuals of archival footage, psychedelic light show, not just during inter-mission but before the show.

I said, "Do you have the visuals?" He answered, "No, I haven't finished them yet." I said, "OK, I'm going to work blind here. All right, I'll give it a shot. How much music do you need?"

He said, "Well there are five shows. I would love it where I have enough music so I wouldn't have to repeat anything."

I counted up the amount of hours, pre-show, set breaks, etc. I came back and asked, "Justin, do you realize you're asking me for five hours of music? That's insane."

He said, "Oh, I didn't realize that. That is a lot. Gee, well, do your best. See what you can do." I agreed. At that point I really had no idea what success would be. An hour wouldn't be enough, two hours wouldn't be enough. I figured I would see if I could do this. Even though it was completely insane with the budget that we had.

Making five hours of feasible music for anyone is really not an easy task. That's about five records' worth of music.

I was in a spot, really, so I thought the first order of business was to get a great band. I got Adam McDougall on keys, Dan Horne on bass, and Mark Levy on drums. We got into the studio and we didn't have much time.

Justin wanted music that felt familiar to The Grateful Dead. If it got too far away from that feel, it would be a disconnect for the crowd. If it was mimicked music, it would be even more annoying. We had to try and strike this balance so it would have that essence. But he didn't want it to sound like a cheap cover band.

We went into the studio for two days with nothing prepared ahead of time. We just went for it. I said, "OK, this is going to have an 'Althea'-ish groove," as in the song by The Grateful Dead. We would get something that felt a little like it, where it would catch your ear, but we wouldn't do the song. We would dance around the theme and take it from there.

Because we had to make so much music, we had to play with a patience that I know I'd never come close to. The pieces of music were 25 minutes long. It's very difficult to play that way, to make your musical events happen many minutes more than you would normally make them happen.

We had to take a very meditative, raga-esque mindset. "This piece of music is going to take a half hour. We're going to be very, very patient here. We're not trying to change the world with this. We're not trying to even excite anyone with this. This is background music without being Muzak. It can't just fall flat on its face. It has to be interesting, but it's going to take a long time."

It was really a mind-melting kind of thing to get into. We only had a certain amount of time, so we were forced into this whole thing. It was similar with CRB when Chris thrust me into this position: "We have shows booked. You're going to figure this out." Same with Fare Thee Well: "You're doing this, and the shows are in three weeks. You have to figure this out."

If we had had time to think this through, it never would have come together. But because it had to happen and quickly, we were forced into this magic situation. Adam was right there with me on this.

We were not sure what it was. We didn't know if it was any good at all. Way too much to take in. And we mixed it very quickly and turned it in to Justin. We didn't see the visuals. We didn't know what anything was going to be. We didn't know if anyone was even going to hear it. We thought it might be like music in a restaurant that nobody pays attention to. You can barely hear it and that's all.

We went to the Santa Clara show on the first gig. Everything changed right there. I was very naive to think that no one was going to hear this. All the music was streaming through computers at home. By the middle of the intermission of the first show, my phone was on fire with texts. "What is this music? We can hear that it's you."

I went to Dead shows in the 80s and 90s. Then this twenty-year period goes by, and all of a sudden there's 80,000 people in the stadium for their first gig back. Anyone who was there knows it was a heart-wrenching, soul-piercing experience. It was very emotional for all of us. Then the rainbow appeared over the stage.

Ears Deeper

Improvisational instrumental music interests me as much as song writing. It's newer territory for me. I've always loved jazz music and I've listened to some Ornette Coleman—I have a large record collection—and it all interests me, because it's all connected and it's all beautiful. But I never really considered myself able to play like that. I always operated in the song world, in the band world, up until the last five or six years, when I became part of this jam world, if you will. I was thrust into it. I didn't go looking for it.

Making instrumental music is an incredible new area of exploration. It's endless what you can do with it. I don't feel as comfortable as some other musicians that are now friends of mine do. I'm friends with some of these incredible guitar players: anyone from Jimmy Herring to Scott Metzger ,to keyboardists like Jeff Chimenti, Erik Deutsch, and Adam MacDougall, to multi-instrumentalists like Jason Crosby. I'm not up to par with them, really. My harmonic depth is extremely limited

I don't have much agility in my guitar playing, I don't have much speed. Not that I have to be a fast guitar player, but a little agility can help get you out of a jam. It's good musical action when you can do it well. Some of my harmonic knowledge is not that deep. I'm too much of a rock player. I need to get my ears deeper.

Circles Around the Sun

This instrumental music that we're making gives me a chance to truly explore with people that I love to play with. Circles Around the Sun is rhythmically based, so you can dance to it.

The other great thing about CATS: at this point I'm not singing, which de-emphasizes my role on stage. The older I get, the less I like being the center of attention. I like being second guy. I can fade into the background, and the primacy of the music can step forward. As time goes on, I'd like to increase visuals, have a nice light show, and have people there to enjoy the experience. Not be looking at me as a singer. I don't have to deliver some kind of message to them, because I don't really have one, other than the love of making music and love of communities. What music can do for people as a community and build communities and just have a good time.

Second in Command

Leadership is big ears. It's truly listening and making a decision to be sympathetic. That's what I'm after.

It depends on what your agenda is in all this. It becomes pretty apparent with most people, after a while you can see exactly what they're up to, even if they're trying to hide it. You can see what they're after and what they're going for. There are some musicians who are focused on themselves, and that's great. In fact, that really works in many cases.

When I was younger, I tried on several identities, tried on a few hats, to see what felt right and what fit. When I try to make it all about me, and here comes my solo and my thing—that never felt quite right. I like being an ensemble player and listening to others and play off of them.

It's really important when I play behind people like Chris or Todd Snider or even Phil Lesh that I'm there for them. I like being the second-in-command, the guy right behind the leader. I like that role and I think it's one of my strengths.

Merely a Student

I'm going to keep on playing music that is interesting to me. Whenever I just let it go and follow my instincts and go for it, that's when the best things happen. That's why Circles Around the Sun happened. We just happened to throw ourselves over a ledge and go. When we did that, it's so beautiful that way, and that's where I'm staying. Hopefully the music that we make will eventually worm its way into wider circles.

The Grateful Dead music at one time was for a very select group of people. No one would have ever predicted the worldwide phenomena that they have become, and that it keeps on growing in these weird ways. When it blew up in the late 80s, people were like "What?!" It got even bigger in the 90s and people were still like "What?!"

Now it's 20 years after they were even a band, and it's even bigger than ever and it's still like "What?!" You never would have thought that thirty years ago.

Maybe Circles Around the Sun will be some legendary thing. Maybe people will forget it next year. Who cares?

I've applied the lessons that I've learned from Grateful Dead music, which is connected to jazz music, and I took the lessons that I learned from Chris and Adam and our late-night hangs on our bus listening to deep jazz records. I took the lessons I learned from George Sluppik, I took the lessons I learned from Tony Leone, and I simply try and represent.

In my mind I'm a pretty crap guitar player. Some people think I'm great, but when I put myself up against the people who I love, I am merely a student. I do have something to offer, I suppose. I'm excited to see where this music goes. I love playing with Adam, and I love Dan and Mark: they're my friends. We're not out there to make a buck, because it is not an established fact that we have any kind of built-in audience. We're going to have to work really hard for whatever we get.

Compensating for What I Can't Do
There's parts of Mel Brown's guitar playing that find I can relate to. He was really a blues player with a lot of speed. He had a cool way of playing fast and he had his own voice on the guitar. He wasn't a genius the way someone like Kenny Burrell is. He was scrappy and bluesy and played in a very idiosyncratic way, that when you hear it you know it's him.

That I can relate to, because I feel similar. I'm a little scrappy. I don't have the virtuoso qualities that I admire so much in others. I do have some personality, got a little moxie, and I find my own way of playing simple things to give it a little bit of my own flair. Some people can tell that it's me. Those are compensatory methods. A lot of times, when you don't have a lot of ability you make up for it with personality. I do that all the time. That's what my style is: it's all compensating for what I can't do.

I get that feeling from him when I hear his records. He had a wild, reckless, almost going-off-the-rails quality to his playing. There's great humor in his playing. That "scratchy" thing he had, it just makes me laugh sometimes. I'm inspired by him a lot, trying to get more humor into my playing.

Check in on That
My load is light, my overhead is low. I don't have a family to support: it's just me. I have a little house that I rent, a few guitars and my record collection, and a lot of good friends. Even being in

my 40s, I was able to pick up and join the Chris Robinson Brotherhood.

It's still that way, except now I'm in all these groups and I tour all the time. If I had more responsibilities, it would be hard for me to do it. At this stage, all this music is my entire life, which may be unhealthy. We may need to check in on that. I'm just doing my best to play for whoever shows up. We're older people playing music. I don't really know who our audience is. I don't even know what young bands even do anymore. I don't know how anyone's going to get by doing anything, honestly.

A Gnawing

While I was surfing a little while ago, I was thinking about how song writing is constantly gnawing at me. The idea of writing songs, and the need to write what I feel are good songs, gnaws at me stronger than almost anything else in life.

Infinite Ways to Live

Other things fade into the background. And when I'm really honest with myself, writing songs, playing music, singing, there is a true need to do it. I don't know if I would "die" if I didn't. I might not die. I might have to figure something else out, because living life is a beautiful thing. I don't want to think that I'd have to die without anything. There's infinite ways to live a life, so maybe something else could be figured out. But I'd rather not face that prospect, that's for sure.

PART 3

WIZARDS

This section of *The Cats!* Volume 1 focuses on wizards of music. Only two letters separate "magic" and "music." These artists make magic on the bandstand.

Many of them had plenty of studio experience but eventually branched off on the tree of music to become leaders and innovators in sound and time.

They have been pioneers of facility and feel. They recognized change in the music and in some cases helped it to change. They did this in a most wizardly fashion, creating a new experience for the listener. For example, a whirlwind of tone color as the music moved from acoustic to electric instrumentation. They saw it as their responsibility to play their music for the people and to serve as role models for a cadre of other musicians who were searching for their own individuality. The wizards were the best scouts, filling up the bandstand with an ear for those who could fill in and eventually take over. With the wizards I spent less time discussing theory and a whole lot of time on values, points of view, trust, and courage.

Most wizards are multi-instrumentalists who never play the same song the same way once. These songs could be from the hills of Appalachia or the concrete jungle of any major urban center of this country. Their musical aptitude encompasses all forms: blues, ragas, bluegrass, free jazz, bayou, psychedelia, and funk.

I wanted to create a platform that opened portals to new information from individuals who have rarely if ever been asked to pontificate on their reality. In my search I realized that I desired to provide a bridge of knowledge for my generation and future communicators. Wizards can do this.

Being able to interview my heroes in music has been a life-affirming process. This venture has been an intergenerational excursion into our cultural history. As I listen back, I can hear my growth as an interviewer, writer, investigator, and human. I feel it is important to share their stories, because they preserve and promote the essence of who we are as humans.

These wizards learned under the masters before them, took the music in a new direction, and got the memo about giving back. Philanthropists of musical knowledge, they lace the music with their own personal touch that creates a meal.

Mason Williams told me in an interview that the great Ken Kesey said, "Almost everybody can be clever, but what you really want to do is try to be magical."

These wizards are magical. Please enjoy this deep well of enlightenment.

LARRY CORYELL

Larry Coryell was a pioneer of electric guitar. Growing up in Washington State, his roots were in Country and Western, but he recognized he needed to learn the language of jazz in order to increase his musical vocabulary. The only way to do this was to move to New York and submerge himself in the scene. He was part of the first fusion band in New York, The Free Spirits, and began his prolific solo career on Vanguard Records.

His first major gig was given to him by Gabor Szabo when he took Gabor's place in Chico Hamilton's band. From there Larry began immersing himself in the fertile New York loft scene, where he met future collaborators such as Randy Brecker, Chick Corea, and Lenny White. All the while Larry kept melding the roots of folk, country, and blues with psychedelic rock and progressive jazz. He became widely popular in Europe through his collaborations with Wolfgang Meltz and Philip Catherine. He's been a leader on dozens of albums and collaborated with Charles Mingus, Herbie Mann, and Stéphane Grappelli.

Larry passed away in February 2017. I was fortunate enough to interview him twice on my radio program: in October 2015 and April 2016. These interviews encompass his concept of jazz, how the Miles Davis film (*Miles Ahead*) revolved around the recording session he did with Miles, how he overcame years of substance abuse, and being part of The Free Spirits.

Beautiful Flowers of Music

Jazz is a music that's harmonically complex and very beautiful. It's a work of art. I remember the first time I heard a solo by Wes Montgomery. It was so beautiful, but I didn't understand it. At the same time, I really loved it. I wanted to know what it was.

It's African-based; it's definitely an African phenomenon. You don't have to be African American to play it. You have to understand it comes from black culture.

It's derived from the way black people hear music and from the way they compose forms. Word forms and hollers and field hollers, which evolved into a blues. The blues was the foundation of all the forms. In jazz it was expressed by Billy Strayhorn, Duke Ellington, and Fletcher Henderson.

It was not just a blues, the way people might think of the blues: B. B. King or something relatively simple. The blues evolved out of a long period of suffering by African American people. It was like out of a muddy, wet dank swamp of culture that made beautiful flowers, which were fertilized from that life of complexity and difficulty. Beautiful flowers of music that were original grew forth out of that mud, like a lotus.

Spear-header

A leader is someone who instills confidence in themselves and the band. Someone who has the wisdom to make the right decisions regardless of what the situation is. You play the percentages.

Herbie Mann is a good example. He was a great band leader. He took care of the people who played his music. He was a gentleman, a cheerleader, a spear-header. He would come up with ideas we could all get behind. He was able to assemble groups of people that seemingly were unrelated to play together. He had a lot of wisdom and really understood music. Take me and Sonny Sharrock with a rhythm section from Muscle Shoals, Alabama. We were playing stuff by Sam & Dave and Aretha Franklin.

Schlock

In high school, I discovered jazz music through one of my guitar teachers. It was a music I did not understand at that time. I didn't know what it was, but I certainly wanted to know how to play it. The jazz life consists of the pursuit of that desire. To learn how to play that music and understand why it is so important and why it is so significant.

If you don't understand the music, you can't play it. I was exposed to a lot of popular music on the radio. A lot of interesting stuff and a lot of shlock. I heard a lot of Country and Western. There was a lot of great guitar playing on those songs. I found out later Chet Atkins did most of those solos. One of the first records I ever bought was a Chet Atkins record.

It Was All Free
By the end of the summer of 1965 I had dropped out of school. I had been playing in what is known as a "commercial band." The musicians were pretty good and the gigs were pretty decent.

I then got my own gig, an organ trio, but I realized I didn't know anything about the music. I knew nothing about jazz music, if the truth were told. People would say, "Hey, you're pretty good." I knew better. All I had to do was listen to myself. I needed to go to where the music was really happening and that was New York. It was fifty years ago this past September.

I arrived in New York and was not disappointed. It was non-stop excitement. In one week I heard more good music than I had in my previous 22 years.

I lived on the Lower East Side and I started finding people who were like me. Unknown musicians who wanted to establish a career. Various people would know where the sessions were; they would take me to them. A lot of them were just jam sessions, where there was not a normal tune being played—it was all free.

Not Really Real
A lot of people were taking LSD and playing. Looking back on it, one acid trip would have been enough. It opened doors to perceiving music from that standpoint. All the other acid trips are just a waste of time. I think it's a very dangerous drug.

I did what I did, and I'm glad it's over. A lot of my experiences were positive, but it's still a drug. It's still artificial. It's not really real.

Every Note was Correct
I was trying so hard to play with Bob Dylan, but Mike Bloomfield got the gig. A little bit after that is when Gary Burton wanted to start his group. He came to hear The Free Spirits and he made a proposal to me. He said the band was going to be Roy Haynes and Steve Swallow. I couldn't really turn *that* down.

Burton was a prodigious musician. A few years before, George Shearing had hired him. There was going to be a record date on a Friday. Thursday night Gary stayed up for a few hours extra and composed and arranged a whole bunch of music. He brought it into the studio the next day and they all played it right on the spot. He's very "Mozartian" in his ways, Mozart was known for being a perfect sight-reader. Every note he wrote on the paper was correct. Gary has a lot of that in him.

The Jazz Life
There was a lot of stuff going on underground in Stuttgart, Germany in the early 70s. Wolfgang Dauner heard me on a record, found me, and asked me to play on his record. It was beautiful and gave me instant enjoyment and respect for the European culture.

Because of Dauner, over the last 50 years I went from being almost an isolated American culturally to somebody who's much more aware of the entire world. I'm writing my second opera. My first opera was based on Tolstoy's *War and Peace*.

I'm getting deep into James Joyce, who I found out was a guitarist. I'm also getting deep into forms of music that use a lot of odd meters. It's really good for your overall education when you embrace "the jazz life."

People in Europe appreciate jazz more. It's a pretty sure guess that a lot of African American musicians wanted to escape the horrible, horrible prejudice. They didn't get that so much in Europe. The first time we went over to France, they gave us such a warm welcome that we didn't want to go back. The first time Charlie Parker was over in Europe, he was having such a great time he never wanted leave. The black musicians didn't get the prejudice they got in America, and the Europeans loved the music almost as much as the Americans did.

Don't Finish Your Phrases

The Miles movie revolves around the recording date that Miles did with me. I'm not mentioned in the film, but that recording Miles produced of me is the focal point of the caper. It's a caper movie. Miles was not active during the time, and according to the movie it was all about trying to get some new product out of Miles.

Teo Macero was there and Miles was there. He had two other synthesizer players there. He had Al Foster on drums. All that week up in Connecticut where he was staying, he was writing the composition and gradually teaching me how I wanted to play it. He would always tell me, "Use more space. Put more holes and don't finish your phrases." That's the best thing I ever learned from him. Never finish a phrase. Miles was great, he wanted to make music and help other cats out.

It was great being mentored by him, although what we did was never released. That's because he didn't play trumpet on it. He only played synthesizer.

How to Get Sober

John McLaughlin and I were initiated the same night with Sri Chinmoy. I converted Carlos Santana within a year or two along with his buddy Tom Costner. Through it all I couldn't stop getting high, so I missed the full benefit of practicing yoga with Sri Chinmoy. The getting-high thing was so fully ingrained in my life habits that it caused a lot of problems.

It stayed this way until the early 80s. I had all these things lined up with Philip Catherine; a lot of money was on the table. That's when I hit rock bottom. It was like CC Sabathia checking into AA. That couldn't have come at a worse time for his team. I knew at this point, even with all the opportunities, I had to go away.

I had gone away four previous times, but I never really understood how to get sober. This fifth time it was really bad, and

I was afraid I was going to die if I didn't get straight. I went in 34 years ago last month. I stayed low, stuck it out, and didn't really focus on anything else other than getting sober.

The spirituality that had branched out from what John Coltrane had inspired us to do in the 60s came later for me. After I had been sober for a year, I realized I wanted to see if I could get a more Eastern orientation to my spirituality. I was converted to Buddhism by Herbie Hancock and Wayne Shorter. I've been practicing that Buddhism for 31 years. I couldn't have done it if I hadn't been alcohol-free and drug-free.

I remember when Bill Evans died, we all went to the memorial service in midtown Manhattan. A buddy of mine and I were lamenting that Bill had passed. He looked at me and said, "Larry, you shouldn't even smoke a joint. You shouldn't take anything."

He had to be on the receiving end of my behavior as an alcoholic. He knew what he was talking about, and when he said that, it was a wake-up call. It's something I couldn't see because all I ever thought about was music.

Very few people can quit based on will power alone. It a major lifestyle change. Sober is a lifestyle; it's different.

LENNY WHITE

Lenny White was 13 years old when his father started taking him to the jazz clubs to see his heroes. Soon thereafter Lenny was on the bandstand with Jackie McLean, getting a baptism by fire. Every night he and his dad would go home late and every morning his dad would head off to work and Lenny to school.

This early apprenticeship emboldened Lenny to develop a mastery of the drum kit. By the late 60s he was recording with Andrew Hill, Joe Henderson, Curtis Fuller, and Miles Davis. His seminal work came on Freddie Hubbard's classic album *Red Clay*.

Lenny went to San Francisco and wound up in the Latin rock band Azteca. While he was with them, Chick Corea pursued Lenny to take over the drum chair in Return to Forever. Eventually Lenny succumbed to Chick's pleadings and that led to a successful run as one of the leading fusion bands of that era. He is considered one of the founding fathers of jazz fusion and is a three-time Grammy award-winning drummer.

I interviewed Lenny twice on my radio show: in January 2014 and April 2015. In these excerpts Lenny and I discuss working in the studio with Miles Davis, how he has kept his music "pure," the differences between his musical education and that of today's students, and being inspired by Roy Haynes.

The Creative Source

When you play something that you don't know where it came from, you play something and someone says, "Man, wow, that was amazing, where did that come from?" And you say, "I don't know," but you know it's coming from another source, a positive source.

I've always been of the belief that if I took any mind-altering substances, then my music wouldn't be pure. I know that comes from a pure place, and when there's things that happen that I play that I don't know how I got that, I know it's coming from another place. It's the music playing me.

Our solutions for coping with whatever problems we have are artistic—even in the sense of self-medication back in the day. I was around a lot of people who did drugs, but I didn't do them. My position has always been that the creative source came through me. Then people got it. If that was the case— where the creative source came through me—I had to be as pure as I could be. I'm not saying that was everybody's attitude—that's my attitude. There were people that did, and there were fantastic creations that came from drugs. That motivation and that mind set to explore brought some really very interesting and seminal creations.

Obligation to Seek

There's been a break in the lineage. When I was coming up, maybe it was easier. There were still masters that were active and around.

All my heroes were alive, and I got the opportunity to see them, speak to them, and be in their presence. I had the opportunities to ask questions about representing the music the right way. I could go out every night and hear the musicians that made these records. Tony Williams brought a different language to the instrument when he played a splash with the high hat and played a five-stroke roll, not just on the snare drum but between bass drum, snare drum, and high hat. You listen to that on a record and you go "Wow." Then you see a guy play that and you go "Whoa, man!" You want to go right back into your basement apartment, put the pads up, and practice what you saw.

That's the difference: I could do that because I saw it. What's happened now is that the music has changed. The actual obligation to represent the music has changed. Because there are more records, there are more people doing this and doing that. There are now many new kinds and new ways of doing things that have become more accepted than the actual real music. When I talk to young musicians, I tell them it's an obligation for them to seek.

A lot of people don't realize that if you start with Tony Williams, you have to go investigate where his sound came from. Younger musicians don't do that enough.

Academia does something to the actual musical experience. Trying to teach methodology in how somebody plays something is one thing, but to get inside their head to formulate *why* they play it, that's what they don't teach in school. They teach the invention, "This is a C chord and these are the things Dizzy Gillespie played over a C chord." They figure if they teach that, then that guy can sound like Dizzy.

The fact is, you have to get inside Dizzy's head, "Why did he choose those notes? What did he listen to, to build his approach." If you teach *that*, then you'll have a trumpet player sounding like Joe Smith that's influenced by Dizzy and has become a great new sound, as opposed to someone sounding exactly like Dizzy because they listened to and transcribed his solo on "Night In Tunisia."

Still Thirsty

When singular people ask questions and those questions get answered but the people are still thirsty, they ask more questions. Then their knowledge expands. When those singular people's knowledge expands and they continue to ask questions, the universe expands. It expands one person at a time. And if we continue to do that, the universe continues to expand.

That is still happening today, but it's not happening the way it did in the 60s. When Steely Dan did *Aja*, when I heard that record, I said "Wow! Pop music has some different chords here, and there are odd meters within the songs." In the 60s that would happen normally, because of the way culture was. Everybody was searching, seeking, and experimenting—in all different aspects of life and culture. If you could change things, you became successful, and you could be rich by coming up with a new formula.

That's not the case anymore. You can become rich doing something everybody does. There's been a big attitude change. Now people are more concerned about surviving. They've made a whole bunch of money and bought a whole bunch of things. Now they're worried about keeping the things that they bought.

It's about "I need to do this so I make money and pay for what I have." That's why people are playing it safe. That's why you can't even get a record deal—not saying that you really want one. You can't get a record deal today without having some sort of mark in the social marketplace. Record companies don't sign artists for their talent but because they have 30,000 followers on Twitter.

It's not an exploratory attitude today. It's more of a corporate point of view about "How can we expand?" As opposed to, "Let's see when we experiment what we can come up with."

Lace the Coffee

I've managed to come across and meet some fantastic new musicians. I've been able to work with them, either in a playing capacity or a producing capacity. These are pop artists or progressive artists that want to make a change in their music. Their music isn't necessarily 4/4 jazz, which is what I came up playing.

They'll still say, "I like what you did back then, and I want to take some of that and put it in my music today. This is how I hear my music today, but I want you to put some of what it is that you did in your generation into my music."

What you get is some pop music that has some sensibilities within it. If you make music that's like cognac, your music will go over very well with cognac drinkers. But if I really wanted to make a change, then I have to take something that everybody drinks. Everybody drinks coffee, so I have to take what I want to do and put it in the coffee. I have to lace the coffee, so people drink the coffee and say, "This is some interesting-tasting coffee. I've never tasted coffee like this before, but it's pretty good."

That's what I would like to attempt to do: to somehow lace pop music till people realize that it is music and "this is different." They're saying something, there's some substance to these lyrics, there's some substance to this groove.

I'm on the road now playing, and people come out to see us play and they're from our generation, Boomers. I say to them, "You guys are fortunate, because you come from the same generation that I come from and you supported what we do, and you've lived in a generation where music meant something. Music that you listened to, that we played, made you dress a certain way, made you think a certain way, made you stand up and take notice of yourself, and say, "I want to make a change."'

No Backbeat

Practice is always great, but when you play with live musicians it's about the application of what you practice. You can't sound like you practice, so you have to make music out of it.

Musical styles in the late 60s, early 70s had morphed, and they morphed into something that was inclusive of all kinds of music that had come before and all kinds of music that were prevalent at the time. You had your soul/RnB, jazz, funk. Later on they called it "fusion." That's somebody's word for something that they can't describe. It stuck, unfortunately.

I'm of the generation where you had to play all kinds of music. You just couldn't get by playing one kind of music. It enriched your perception of music, because you had to be inclusive of everything. You had to listen to everything, put it together and make it work.

When I first played with Jackie McLean, I met him on the bandstand. He turned around, said "Hello," and called out a tune. I didn't know the tune. I played through it and said to myself, "OK, this is a baptism by fire. This is it, this is real. I'm no longer in my basement practicing to records, this is real." I was 17 years old.

I played a backbeat on the bandstand with Jackie McLean. He turned around and yelled at me, "No backbeat, no backbeat." I learned by making mistakes or failing at something. You know the next time you cannot do that. You know what to do next time to save you from the same mistake.

Early on in someone's career, if they're mistake-free it might haunt them later on, because they might be limited in what it is that needs to be done.

I learned from band leaders telling me, "Hey, man, that's not what you play." I remember doing my first live gig with Ron Carter. He played something that was off of the beat and I did the same thing. He said, "Man don't do that. If you do that, that negates what it is I'm doing. You have to play something, so that I can play against what it is that you do, to make what it is that I do interesting."

I learned the hard way, but those things stuck in my brain. Now I teach the same way.

You Ain't Getting' The Chicken

My parents and my peers taught me that you have to be representative to what it is you're going to do. If you are not on point, then you need to get on point. Learning to play a session and hearing the bandleader say "Next!"

The only time this ever happened to me was with Miles when we made *Bitches Brew*. We were doing this tune "Miles Runs the Voodoo Down." Now there are outtakes that I have had the opportunity to hear which I played on that I think sound killin'. Miles wanted something different: a little more of a funky groove. Now, I had played more funk music than anybody on that session, but because Tony Williams was God Drums to me—he played with Miles, now I'm playing with Miles—that's what I thought Miles wanted. So I'm playing, and it sounds good to me. Miles came over and whispered in my ear, "You ain't gettin' the chicken." Don Alias came over and started playing this really simple beat. I couldn't believe I let this opportunity go 'cause I wanted to be slicker than what Miles wanted me to do.

After the session—I wound up playing shekere and percussion—and I'm sitting over in the corner. Miles comes over and says, "Hey, man, what's up?" I replied, "You know I wanted to get it right on that tune." He said, "Man, don't even worry about it. Be back here tomorrow morning at 10." It was great. Don't worry about it!

The Master

One of the defining moments for me was when Roy Haynes was playing at Slugs. He knew of me and knew that I was playing and championed me forever. I will always be indebted to him.

At the end of every set, Roy would play the "Negro National Anthem," which is "Lift Every Voice and Sing."

They'd play it and go "Dah, dah, dah, dah." Then he'd play a solo. He's playing on stage and he goes, "Dah, dah, dah, dah," and puts down the sticks. He points at me and says, "Come on up and play."

I come up and I play the solo. Then he gets back on the drums and goes, "Dah, dah, dah dah." This is Master Roy Haynes! The fact that he did that was so great to me that it was life-changing.

DAVE LIEBMAN

Dave Liebman is a saxophonist who learned under the masters of music. He was a white kid participating in a black subculture through much of the 1960s and 70s.

Coming up in the venerable loft scene of the West Village in Manhattan, Dave cultivated his own sound by playing with his peers, including Randy Brecker, Steve Grossman, and Dave Holland. After a stint with the power horn band known as Ten Wheel Drive, Dave had a chance to play with Miles Davis and Elvin Jones. He has always tried to pay homage to the cats by merging jazz with spiritual music. Taking standard tunes and taking them as far out as they could go, with Tisziji Muñoz or Pee Wee Ellis, or in his own group, Lookout Farm.

Aside from touring and recording, Dave has been working at universities throughout the United States to help students find their own sound, be good leaders, and sustain a living as improvisational musicians.

I did a radio interview with Dave in April 2016. In it we talk about the Zen leadership qualities of his mentors, the relevance of a jazz education now, being the first white band on the Motown label, and how music has healed him and kept him together.

Specifically Healing

I am (and we are) fortunate to have the music; without it I don't know what I'd do. Music *is* a healing force; it's obvious that it's coming from another source beyond the material world. From Mozart to Jimi Hendrix to John Coltrane, etc., it's all coming from outside of our physical being.

Improvised music is specifically healing because it's in the moment combined with the vibe that is being felt between you and your audience and the musicians. Even if you don't have an audience, you have a vibe. We're very fortunate, those of us who play this music and do it for a living and are recognized enough to be able to continue. We're very, very fortunate to live a life like that. You're kind of a medicine man; it's shamanism to me. In the end that's what it is, that's what we do.

Playing for the Door

I think a jazz education is like a really good liberal arts education,, except about music. But the present reality and practicality of a jazz degree is not right—like a young person accumulating $200,000 in debt? On my side, we're living, being able to teach. This hypocrisy, if that's what you want to call it, is very upsetting, if you think about it the way we're talking. You're not going to put your money in that style. Jazz has an incredible history—a living history with some of the original masters still around. On the other hand, how are you going to do it if you're going to "play for the door"? You can't ignore what's going on, when the reality of playing for the door is obvious.

Our loft jam sessions in the late 60s and early 70s were the equivalent of guys showing up for an ensemble at Arizona State at 3:00 pm. OK, not quite the same atmosphere or "accoutrements," but it's guys playing in a situation where somebody brings in music to play and so on. We were very enamored of Coltrane's *Ascension* and *Interstellar Space*. That affected us and inspired the free jazz a lot of us began with before learning bebop, etc. I'm talking late Trane, Cecil Taylor, Ornette Coleman, and others.

Pre-Bop

We have to play to make points. In the end whatever we teach or say is secondary to the process of being on the stage with somebody who is more experienced. When they get on stage, they start to feel the timing, the drama/storytelling, inflection, attitude—all the stuff you really can't teach. Until the student actually gets on stage with musicians of another generation, they're not really going to get it.

These days with the masters being pretty much gone, most of the young musicians play with other young musicians. That has its advantages and disadvantages. Experience, of course, is lacking in that respect.

Accessing the source of the music was not as easy coming up in my time as it is now. Today you can press a button and have a history of music in front of you on a phone. I was not familiar with pre-bop at all. Lennie Tristano, who I studied with for one year, made me sing Lester Young solos from famous Count Basie recordings from the late 30s. That was my first formal introduction to pre-bop. In those days, if you didn't have somebody laying it on you, you didn't really get it, because there was no formal teaching. You got it by hit and miss. Someone would say: "Hey did you hear this Duke Ellington record, *Money Jungle*? You ought to check it out." It's a process and it's beautiful!

Heavy Gig

If you're on the bandstand and you're a good student (which I am), you're going to be observing everything that's happening: physically, mentally, spiritually, and of course musically. You go to those who have experience, who have been there before you, are senior to you, and hopefully they'll be generous enough to share their experience and their knowledge. When you watch somebody play, you say, "I need to do that." That is the message of the day.

I knew I was in a special honored and fortunate position to be on the stage with these people. Everything they did, I watched and imitated. Without verbal guidance, it would be more "Look at the way he played that. Look at the way he did that. Look at how he said that. What tune did he call? Why'd he call that?" I tried to follow everything I could from them, because I knew this was knowledge that was never going to happen again for me. Then you go back and think about it. I believe part of the forming of your own personality is the way you hear something, because the way you hear it may not be the way the guy said it. You might be hearing it in your particular peculiar way, which in the end becomes who you are.

Pete La Roca was a drummer in the 60s who was my first mentor. He eventually quit the business and became a lawyer. Over the years, I played with him on different occasions. He was quite influential on my life. My first real heavy gig at 23 years old.

Sawbuck

I wasn't enough of a player to make a living playing jazz. So when I got out of college, finishing with a degree in American history, I taught public school. When I got hired by Ten Wheel Drive, there was a weekly salary, so I stopped teaching. I was the main soloist, which meant I did improvise a bit. Part of the horn-band premise was that there were going to be at least some improvised solos. It was the beginning of fusion, meaning you had a rock beat with an improvised solo over it. That gig led into another band which eventually got signed to Motown. I believe Sawbuck, under its new name, Gotham, was the first white band on Motown.

At the same time Elvin Jones hired me and I moved back into jazz. This was my path, from free jazz to a backbeat to Elvin and then Miles Davis, which went back to the backbeat because of the style, *On the Corner*, in the 70s. I got lucky!

The Next Forty Years

I had many mentors, mainly Pete, Elvin, and, of course, Miles. They each had their own particular way of doing things, both on and off the bandstand. Real individualists, which is a pretty good way to discuss jazz musicians as people. Pete was quite an intellectual and very smart. He could explain things to you in detail. Elvin was not that verbal about the music itself, but he was an amazingly beautiful person and of course player. Miles said hardly anything. You had to decipher the code. It was a subculture. The jazz world was unique, mostly African American till the 70s. You were entering a whole other way of thinking, certainly speaking, and of course making a living. There was a lot to be gleaned just from innuendo and nuance and your imagination. I think those guys were all Zen-like.

I have my quotations from each of these masters that I use for teaching. I'll say: "This is what I thought of that then, and this is what I think of it now." They didn't say: "Play that, play this." They said: "Play like I do or watch me."

There's nothing like living the process of on-the-spot, in-the-moment learning. There's nothing like that. Even listening to a record is remote until you're on the stage in the heat of the battle. Each of these gentlemen (and others too numerous to list) gave me words of different depths. I'd take something home and think: "What did he really mean by that?" You didn't go back to ask these guys; this was not the scene. You said "thank you" and thought about it for the next forty years!

Past the Point

Miles told me one time: "Stop before you're done." He always left a lot of space and let the rhythm section conclude what was being said or, even better, instigate the next statement. In order for that to happen, you have to leave space in the music. You literally have to stop playing. His statement was hinting at the fact that you probably were past the point of having finished what you played but kept going—something like that. It becomes unnecessary to add more. Plus it opens the rhythm section up, so that they now have a little space and maybe can do something that you can jump on. I think that's what he meant by that, but it took a minute to understand it.

I found that if you do leave a little space, if you drop the last few bars of a chorus if it's a tune that has a form, and let the rhythm section do something, they will inevitably say to themselves: "Oh, he wants me to do something!"

KENNY BURRELL

Kenny Burrell's roots are in Detroit, but that was only the beginning of his journey. While at Wayne State, he started recording with the late great Dizzy Gillespie. This was followed by stints with Oscar Peterson, John Coltrane, Jimmy Smith, and Kenny Dorham. He has recorded as a leader on the heavy jazz and blues labels such as Chess/Cadet, Prestige, Muse, Verve, and Concord.

By the early 1970s, on top of his busy playing schedule, Kenny started doing college seminars, including the first regular course held in the US chronicling the music of composer, pianist, and bandleader Duke Ellington.

Kenny's unpretentious and practical style has helped galvanize knowledge and wisdom for a generation of up-and-coming musicians who did not experience the breakfast sessions in Atlantic City or Mean Old Frisco, or music before the breakdown of idioms. As Duke said, "It's all music."

Today Kenny is Distinguished Professor of Music and Ethnomusicology and director of the Jazz Studies Department at UCLA. I interviewed him in March 2013. We talked about the street-scholar mentality of Detroit, telling your story through your playing, and his mission now as it relates to elevating the musicians who play this art form.

Be Who You Are

Jazz is great American music, and the musicians are not treated as great American musicians. Part of my mission now and in the future is to try and help correct that idea. To try to gain more respect for the music and the musicians. That will help not only recognize and accept the past but have a better future for what's going on.

There is an unwritten understanding, a credo, in jazz, because the essence of jazz is improvisation: "Be who you are." Grant Green, Wes Montgomery, and John Coltrane: they had their own individual voices. I had the great fortune of playing with all of them.

Grant and I became friends. I was a few years older than him, but when he came to New York we used to have little friendly guitar battles around town. I liked him very much as a person and I loved his music. Unfortunately, he had some drug problems, and the fact that the business, in so many ways, is not kind to jazz musicians didn't help anything. I feel really bad that "here's another victim of these circumstances."

Blues Right Beside Me

When I was 7, 8, 9 years old, I really loved music and my brother was already playing the guitar. In our house in Detroit there was music all around. My mother played piano and my father liked to pick up a ukulele and pluck. Finally, we got a radio and I was listening to Count Basie and Duke Ellington and I really loved the saxophone.

I was watching my brother play the guitar and I thought, that's no big deal. I could play a few chords, so it didn't seem like too much of a challenge.

During World War II my father passed, so there was no real money around. We could not afford a saxophone, so that dream had to be put aside. I reluctantly got a guitar, because I wanted to do something. I bought my first guitar for $10 at a pawn shop, $5 of which was sent to me by my brother Billy, who was in the army. That began the road for me down guitar lane.

At that time I heard Charlie Christian, who was playing the guitar like a saxophone anyway, with the amplifier. I said, "The guitar isn't so bad," so I stuck with it and I started to hear guys like Oscar Moore; and all along the blues was there, sitting right beside me.

More Than We Realized

I went to Wayne State and majored in theory and composition. Tommy Flanagan and I were best friends and we worked together all around Detroit. I was in a group with Tommy, Donald Byrd,

Pepper Adams, and Elvin Jones. We had a little jazz club where we would have jam sessions every month, every Monday night, at this actor's theater. We had jam sessions at each other's homes. Jazz was cool and we just wanted to play. We didn't care who the leader was. Whoever got the gig was OK.

That was like a school, because we were learning from each other. We were buying music, we were exchanging music, we were transcribing a lot off of records. We couldn't buy a lot of the music that we print today. The students now, they can buy anything: you can get everything online.

Growing up in Detroit, there weren't even the books to transcribe the melodies. We had to do that ourselves. In the process you begin to learn and understand what's really going on. It takes time to digest what you are transcribing. You're getting a theory lesson in harmony and melody as you're doing this. You can also kind of understand what that musician is thinking about. We were learning more than we realized. Now there is almost too much to choose from. It's our job and our mission to help the students discern what is important in terms of jazz repertoire.

I had a really good band at the time and Yusef Lateef was in my group at one point; so was Pepper Adams. I remember encouraging Yusef to go and get his degree and also start playing the flute. He did all of that and the result is history. He later became Dr. Lateef. I always feel good that I encouraged him to do that. He was an older student going back to school, but it paid off so well for him.

Yusef Lateef was ten years older than me, and Barry Harris is ten years younger than me. When I went to Miller High School in Detroit, it was great because the music teacher, Mr. Cabrera, knew I was interested in writing. He gave me some great private lessons. So much so that when I went to college and majored in music theory, for the first couple of years I didn't have any homework, I was so prepared.

I was very active in Detroit. Tommy and I were best friends and we played a lot of gigs. I grew up with Donald Byrd and Pepper

Adams and Elvin Jones. The group coming up behind us, the next generation, was Barry Harris's. Ten years before I got there, Yusef Lateef went to that high school with my brother, Billy Burrell, who was my first guitar teacher.

Street Whistling

Everybody whistles. I don't know if you've ever been to New York when the streets are not busy, and you're walking down one of those streets with all the buildings on the side, you get an immediate sound, a special sound in New York, like no other place. It has a reverberation, and that's what made me do that on the album. *Asphalt Canyon Suite* is an image dedicated to New York; that's what Manhattan represented. You can be in your apartment and hear people in the street whistling. I wanted to connect that sound with the city. Not leave jazz, but put a sound in there that would be more directly associated with real life in the streets.

If You Don't Speak up

Jim and Andy's was a bar where a lot of studio musicians would hang out. Oftentimes they were jazz players as well. It was around 54th Street between Broadway and 8th. It was also on 48th Street near 6th Avenue for a while. It had great food and was great for cats that had maybe two or three record dates a day.

I was very fortunate to do pretty much what I was OK with, in terms of plans for recording. If you don't speak up for what you believe in, you're not going to get it. There were several times when I had to really speak up, sometimes in very strong terms, sometimes very diplomatically. That's the way it is, because different people have different priorities. A musician has one and maybe the A&R guy or record producer has another. If they have a disagreement, so be it. I always remembered it's my name on the record, not the person I'm having a problem with. Maybe they need to produce a certain amount of sales or they would lose their job. It's worth fighting for, because your reputation is on the line when you make a recording. I tried to make sure I did what I believed in.

What are people going to think when they hear the record?

Where's Your Story?

You're not going to be like other people anyway, so people don't expect a jazz artist or a blues artist to sound like some somebody else. You have your own story to tell in terms of blues, even if you grow up in suburbia. If you have something to say, it can be important.

You can't expect youngsters to replicate the sound of John Lee Hooker. Some kids try. They learn that, but the real blues fans are going to say, "Well, where's your story?" It's the same thing with jazz.

That's what it's basically all about, and thank God for the people, because the business has a tendency to manipulate things to where people get confused. Overall, I think people are smarter than we give them credit for.

It's a beautiful rich history in this country. That's part of my mission as a teacher: not just help the students play better and find their own voice, but also create an audience that appreciates all of this stuff.

GREG ERRICO

To believe that you were part of real movement towards social progress is validation to some. For those who were actively involved in cultivating the spirit of the change, that is magical. When the involvement is through rhythm, then the spirit transcends.

Greg Errico came from one of the greatest regional hotbeds of local music, the San Francisco Bay. He was the drummer for Sly and the Family Stone, which fashioned the intent of the members—multiethnic, multiracial, male and female—to expose the City by the Bay as a place of experimentation, intellectualism, and a downright fuck-you to American conformity.

Greg moved on from the Family and made stops along the way with Carlos Santana and some of the greatest Afro-Cuban percussionists, including Victor Pantoja, Willie Bobo, Michael Carabello, Armando Peraza, and Coke Escovedo—guys who were rooted in the rhythms made popular by Bay Area vibraphonist Cal Tjader—from Latin Rock to Weather Report and Joe Zawinul's "Boogie Woogie Waltz." While inhabiting fusion, he was also tied to the Novato scene, contributing to *The Apocalypse Now Sessions* at The Barn with Mickey Hart and Bill Kreutzmann. This ultimately paved the way for a connection with Jerry Garcia that lasted nine years.

I've interviewed Greg Errico twice on my radio show: in May 2013 and 2016, and we did a Facebook Live in March 2018. Among the topics discussed are: how he joined Weather Report, his relationship with Joe Zawinul, how or how not to handle fame, the improvisational nature of Sly Stone, and how to approach the groove when you lose the 1 (downbeat).

Looked Like A Kid

I wasn't there for Michael Shrieve's performance at Woodstock, but we all went down to LA for the screening of the movie. I went with all the guys from Santana, and for some reason, Vincent Price the actor was on the plane with us. This was one of those plane flights that had, let's say, an incident. This was in the early days of the 747 Jumbo Jet. Just before we landed in LA, we turned into the flight path of a 747 that was in front of us and we got jet blast from the "wash." It threw our plane out of the sky. I remember Carabello running into the bathroom, and when he came out he was white. It was scary. We hit the ceiling. We got thrown all over the place. It was frightening. Fortunately, no one got hurt.

I remember Michael's drum solo. He looked like a kid. He looked younger than his age to begin with. He did a great performance and it connected with so many people. He still carries that great performance today.

Subject to all the Same Stuff

How you handle fame and all that comes with it being the biggest challenge. It's not an easy thing. You can see the trail of artists who had extreme successes and then had trouble dealing with that success. The money, the attention, the speed with which you travel every day: it's a lot, and there's no book of instruction on it. There's no one teaching you; you're on your own. I walked away from music because it got to a point where I didn't want to become a victim. I wasn't a superstar or anything. I was in a huge group that had a lot of attention and visibility. Still, I was subject to all the same stuff. I was partying and carrying on with everyone, too.

It gets back down to common sense: you just got to know when to draw the line (when you're over it and able to say, "OK, this isn't good anymore"). A lot of times you get into a situation where you're not conscious of it because you're so inebriated—whether drunk or high or in the moment—over these really intense things that are going on. You could become a victim.

Found its Way to Daylight

I started a family at one point, and as music moved into the whole "disco thing" it went to a place where I wasn't needed very much, nor was I that interested. At one point in the 1980s, some brainy producer at Columbia said, "We've got to make 'Dance to the Music' into disco." They took the masters they had of Larry Graham and Errico off of the track and put some disco thing on there. It never found its way to daylight. But I went somewhere else in my life at that time, 'cause music just didn't seem that interesting anymore.

What inspired me to play music again is when the Internet came around. A friend of mine and a big fan of Sly did a website on SATFS. He got ahold of all of us and at the same time he came out, got me a computer, and showed me how to use it: email, etc. As things moved along, I would get emails from fans, and I'd get these letters about how the music we created back in the day inspired people to become drummers, or to love music, or it changed their life. It was just regular honest people telling their stories about how this music we created back in the 60s moved them. Before that, artists would have fans, but you would never have that opportunity for a one-on-one connection. I didn't know that and it was extraordinary. You start looking at what you did again, because it's there to look at. Looking at it from a different perspective and going, "Wow, that's cool." It inspired me to get back into it and connect with it again. Here I am today, full bore. I love it as much or more, playing the music, as I did back then.

Out the Window

With Sly and the Family Stone we used to rehearse and learn stuff—specific. There was a whole map. But when we performed, all was out the window. You had to know it. But once you knew it, then you could forget it and do whatever you're going to do with it. Every time we performed, it was a little different. If you're with people and you know you're on the same page and know you can trust one another, you can go anywhere and all land at the same place at the same time. You could take a mistake and turn it into, actually something that's kind of great. "How'd you do that?" "I don't f***ing know."

In regard to recording with Sly, we would just jam and something might come up: a line, a figure, a feel, a beat. Then we would develop that. A lot of times the tracks were created before the storyline, before the lyric. Sly would go home and listen to the tapes and a thought would come to his head: a line or a sentence. One time, David Kapralik said, "Well, Sly, everyday people." He was referring to something in the conversation. Sly froze in his tracks, picked up a matchbook, and wrote "Everyday People." Then he built the song around those two words.

Sometimes it would happen with a concept, sometimes with words, sometimes with a phrase. There's no rules when it comes to creating like that. It comes every which way, shape, and form.

Spiritually Correct

If you're going in with an understanding that any note can be the 1, the group of people that you're with have to have the same mindset. In a loose sense, if you don't know where the one is, keep your day job. I've seen examples in fusion music with, for example, Billy Cobham when he came out with Mahavishnu. There's a guy who would be playing in seven, eleven, twelve. Odd time signatures or a combination of time signatures; a bar of seven, a bar of twelve. You see that especially in Eastern music.

That's a learned thing. You can learn that technically. But I say to do it proficiently you need to also have a feel for it, a natural feel. There are cats who can take it out there, do a fill in odd time, or elongate the fill and you're going "Holy shit, where's the 1?" You're falling off a cliff and they bring it right down.

The audience isn't necessarily counting, because they usually can't. There is a natural sense of when you really know you bring everybody back in, in the right place. Then there's the other school where it's an improvised thing. It may have gotten lost, but the point is everybody came back in together. That's all that matters. If you could slow it down and count every little thing that happened and say this was mathematically correct, or it could be spiritually correct.

Weather Report

Doug Rauch was hanging out with Miroslav Vitous. Doug was living with me at the time. He wanted to invite Miroslav down to the house to jam with us. And he came. He brought his upright bass and his fender bass a few times. I found him a really intriguing, great guy. Miroslav stopped by one afternoon and said, "Hey, we need a drummer with the Weather Report. Joe Zawinul, Wayne Shorter, and I are going out. We need a drummer. Would you like to do it?"

I said, "Yeah, sure, OK." It came up real quick. At the time I had heard of this group but I wasn't that familiar with the music. I was just going on my vibe with Miroslav.

I'm forever grateful that I did; they're all great people. Absolutely incredible musical experiences, going to places I never would be able to go without doing that.

The whole experience was different from Sly and The Family Stone. We were all over Italy, Europe, Japan. We did the States, too. I had just finished Betty Davis' record about a year before.

I met Joe Zawinul through Miroslav, and we went back to New York. There was a date at Carnegie Hall. We did a show with Deodato. He just had that hit "Also sprach Zarathustra" from *2001: A Space Odyssey*. We hit the stage running. This was a group you were able to do that with: to just jump in, flow with it. I had that ability, so I just had a phenomenal learning experience.

My rehearsal with Weather Report was incidental; more about meeting Joe and hanging. Staying up all night; whatever we did to hang out and talk and connect. All I needed to know musically was the intro and end of a tune. What happened in between was totally what happened in between, that moment. You have to have confidence in the people, a feel for their personalities. The rehearsal was "This is more a taste of what it's going to feel like."

Traveling with Sly Stone, everywhere we'd go would be fast. I like to stop, hang out and go into it, absorb it, and feel what that part of the world is like. With Joe we'd go to a bar; he used to love his cognac. When we were in New York, he would take me to all the jazz clubs, and I would meet all the cats sipping on their cognac. He once introduced me to Dizzy Gillespie.

I got to see Joe perform about six months before he passed, at the Palace of Fine Arts in San Francisco. It was just an extraordinary concert. Afterwards we went out for dinner, then I dropped him off at his hotel. That was the last time I saw him.

STEVE SWALLOW

Steve Swallow is the consummate teammate on the bandstand and a master musician. He has big ears and is always listening and looking to further the musical conversation.

His apprenticeship on the bandstand started in the black clubs in New Haven with T-Bone Walker and Buddy Guy. Upon moving to New York, Steve could be found in the wholesale flower district playing bebop before sunup with Sonny Clark at W. Eugene Smith's celebrated loft.

He became one of the most in-demand studio and live upright bassists, keeping and spending time with Jimmy Giuffre, Paul Bley, Stan Getz, and Gary Burton.

It was at a NAMM show with Gary that Steve first connected with the electric bass. It was love at first touch, and Steve has tried to be an advocate for the electric bass in all musical settings. His passion and dedication to his equipment has continued in his collaborations with his wife, the keyboardist and bandleader Carla Bley.

Steve produced the Scholastic Records sensation *44th Street Portable Flower Factory* with Bob Dorough and cooked the groove on Lowell Levinger's Racoon Records while living in Bolinas.

I have done two radio interviews with Steve: in December 2017 and March 2018. The conversations revolve around his musical roots in the ghettos of New Haven, how the line between blues and jazz didn't exist when he started out, his love affair with the electric bass, Eugene Smith's loft, and learning how to expand his musical palette.

Finding Your Mate

Love is irrational—the electric bass grabbed me by the neck and there it was. It's been a long learning process to get the electric bass to respond under my hands in a way that integrates it within the jazz rhythm section, with a drummer who's playing "ding, dink a ding" on the cymbal instead of "boom, boom, Chak." It's definitely a life's work. I had no choice but to take it on. I didn't want to change the idiom. I was thoroughly devoted to playing jazz music, but with this strange instrument in my hand. I've had to learn techniques that allow the electric bass to function well in the context of the jazz rhythm section. I've also had to seek out guys who make instruments and to try and get them to accommodate my needs. The Fender bass is a remarkable instrument. It's astonishing how much Leo Fender got right in the early 50s, when the Fender Precision and the Fender Jazz Bass first came on to the market. They're remarkably efficient machines. They play low notes with extraordinary efficiency, which is more that can be said of the acoustic bass. The acoustic bass is full of the kind of personality that makes it difficult to play with a major scale over two octaves with each note shaped exactly like its predecessor and the one that follows. The electric bass can do that; the acoustic bass can't do that.

On the other hand, every acoustic bass has a singular personality. Part of what's the wonderful journey of an acoustic bass player is finding your instrument, finding in effect your mate.

There are of course differences between one Fender Precision and another, but essentially you can buy a sound. You can go to the music store and buy a Fender Precision and sound a little bit like "Duck" Dunn or Rocco Prestia.

I remember the first time I heard Jimi Hendrix: it was a revelatory experience. I was driving in a van with Larry Coryell and Gary Burton going across the Golden Gate Bridge. You couldn't get more dramatic than that. "Purple Haze" came on the radio, and electric music got a lot bigger for me. By the time we reached the end of the Golden Gate Bridge I'd been captured. The environment was shifting at that time, and the possibility of playing the electric bass was opening up for the first time.

Jazz music and the rock and roll of that time were coexisting to a certain extent: to a greater extent than they do now. The Burton band I was in opened for Cream and The Electric Flag at The Fillmore in San Francisco.

We played The Fillmore West first before there was the East. Bill Graham was well aware of the young jazz bands that were rising up at that time, in the mid-60s. He, very often, at The Fillmore West would have a three-band bill. He would make the opening band a jazz band; the two succeeding bands were rock and roll bands. It was a revelation just to hear the volume at which Cream plays. I'd never heard music that loud before.

Jack Bruce knew his way around jazz vocabulary, Eric Clapton did not. Eric was a blues player with no jazz in there. Jack and Ginger Baker both had played at Ronnie Scott's jazz club in London, England and were crossing back and forth between those communities, as were many people at that time. The Burton band was experimenting with vocabulary that was foreign to the pure post-bop idiom that was going on at that time. Then again, so was Cannonball Adderley's band. It was a time when distinctions between musics were breaking down or being broken down forcefully.

Benign Hubbub

Political order relies on an atmosphere of restraint. Jazz music at its best discourages restraint. The occasion in which jazz music is played, or in which I play jazz music, today is not unlike the context in which so-called classical music was played. The context in which jazz music is appreciated has changed. People write doctoral theses about it.

That being said, Lester Young and Charlie Parker were among the greatest intellects of the twentieth century—there's no doubt about that. The context in which they arose was not the academy at all. There's a disconnect there, and I don't know what to make of that.

At jazz concerts people sit in chairs, neatly arranged in rows and applaud on cue. When I began playing the music, I was playing in bars where people were into each other as much as they were into the music. That was not an offense in the least. There was a benign hubbub going on in the nightclubs in the late 50s and early 60s that created a very permissive atmosphere on the bandstand. You really got the feeling you could play anything, because the club was there for all kinds of other reasons. It was there to facilitate various sexual rituals and a nexus of political/social activity of all sorts. Jazz clubs were community centers and, unfortunately, I think communities now lack these centers. Or the centers that are serviced by jazz music have certainly shifted. The audience is almost unanimously white, for one thing. That's a curious thing. I watched that shift happen.

Obviously, the phone rings and somebody hires you to play a gig. You do the gig. You watch the terms shift without the sense that you can do anything about it.

He Walked the Bar

The conversation for me started before I moved to New York. I was going to school in New Haven, Connecticut. In the late 1950s there was a remarkably benign music scene going on in the ghetto of New Haven. The main street in that black ghetto was Dixwell Aveue and it was lined with clubs.

Those clubs were filled with rhythm sections and organ trios, piano trios, horn players, passing through all the time. There was a community scene that flourished in all the cities, large and small, in the United States at that time.

It continued to do so into the late 60s, when that scene in the black community got snuffed out dramatically by the time of the riots. The riots hit small businesses in the ghettos in all the cities in America hard. It dealt a death blow to the minority clubs that had thrived until that time.

I was going down to these clubs and playing all night long. It did a lot to further my exit from school. There was a fluent interchange between idioms going on. The vocabularies were cross-referencing all the time. The early RnB drummers like Panama Francis were veterans of the big-band scene. They just kind of moved into the recording studio because there was a window of opportunity there. There was money to be made and the music wasn't bad, it wasn't inauthentic.

It wasn't exactly jazz, but it was deeply moving, heartfelt music. There was no dishonor in playing that music at all. I'm deeply grateful that I experienced that, just as I'm sure John Coltrane was grateful that he walked the bar at one time. It's good for you.

I played with T-Bone Walker and Buddy Guy. The line between blues and jazz didn't really exist in my life mind at that time. T-Bone and Buddy had been plucked out of the Chitin Circuit. In fact, the tours that I did with them were organized by George Wein. It was the early days of his "concert empire," and he had all this diversified beyond what was strictly "jazz" music.

We toured Europe and across the States. Throughout the 60s there was still a market for jazz that has shrunk persistently since. I feel it's an inhalation/exhalation thing and we're due for an exhale any day now.

My Snobbism

I wasn't at all into Elvis Presley or Little Richard. I turned my back on that stuff from about the age of 11 or 12 when I discovered jazz, and that was it for me. At that time, in the early 60s, there was a clear decision you had to make: if you liked jazz, you didn't like Elvis. It wasn't, in fact, until I was 30 years old and started playing the electric bass that I felt obliged to go back and listen to source material to see what other electric bass players were doing. I discovered there was a whole lot of music in there that was worthy of my interest. My snobbism as a jazz musician had been unfortunate and blinded me to some music that was worthy of consideration.

The music that was being played in those clubs in New Haven was essentially bebop-vocabulary music with a lot of blues in it. It wasn't rock and roll, it wasn't Elvis, and it wasn't even Little Richard, who was a lot closer in spirit and practice to the organ trios that lined the clubs on Dixwell Avenue.

When I discovered the electric bass, I went out and bought a bunch of Motown Records with the intention of checking the bass players out, and ended up listening raptly and avidly, not to the bass players, but to Marvin Gaye singing. Marvin and Otis Redding were the two that affected me most strongly; they phrased so beautifully.

Fresh Flowers

Sonny Clark was around when I first came to New York. His touch on the piano would just melt your heart in an instant. He was a magnificent player and absolutely incapable of ordering his life to the extent that you could say, "Sonny, I've got a gig for you. You have to be at Birdland Tuesday at 9 pm." It was absurd that he would make that, but he showed at the session places and the loft places that were open for playing at any time in those days. He would sit down and play brilliantly for a couple of hours and wander away.

In the late 50s and early 1960s, W. Eugene Smith's loft was a focal point for jam sessions. This was a building where Hal Overton, the composer, had a floor, and rehearsals for the Thelonious Monk Town Hall Band took place. There were sessions going on all day and all night in that loft, and several others that were up and down 6th Avenue. Ronnie Free, the drummer, was a denizen at one time. He was the nominal renter of the loft that was Ground Zero for sessions and where I played with Sonny Clark on several occasions. It was the flower district, where wholesale flower companies had their shops. At 7:00 in the morning, the trucks would arrive from the countryside and dump off tons and tons of fresh flowers. This wonderful scent would rise up to the lofts. We'd be, at that point, just about finishing up for the night. Life began around 5 pm, when this part of Manhattan would fall silent, when the businesses who were there would close up, and the people would go home.

All of a sudden. another New York would rise up. It was those of us who stayed up all night learning how to play music. It was a wonderful enchanted environment in the Chelsea neighborhood of Manhattan at that time.

See Sam Stephenson, *The Jazz Loft Project: Photographs and Tapes of W. Eugene Smith from 821 Sixth Avenue, 1957–1965* (New York: Alfred A. Knopf, 2009) and the documentary by Sara Fishko, *The Jazz Loft According to W. Eugene Smith* (2016).

Fatuous to Claim

I knew several people who were strung out, and I saw the danger of getting strung out, and I saw the liabilities associated with that life. On the other hand, I saw these guys were completely committed to junk; there was something about it that was really compelling to them. Objectively I was weighing the two columns on the page, and it seemed to make sense to me to survive. I had the clear sense that I was a late bloomer as well, that it was going to take me a long time to get good at what I was doing, and I would be cutting my life short if I committed to that addiction.

I think it would be fatuous to claim that I made a strong decision not to become addicted. I just kind of lucked out. I managed to avoid it, or it managed to avoid me—hard to say.

The generation before mine, the guys who were ten years older than I was (born in the 1930s): that generation was decimated by heroin. My generation began to pull back from it, and I think it's become increasingly less prevalent in the music community as it's become more prevalent in society in general.

I knew Albert Stinson; he was a friend and also a heroin addict. I last saw him shortly before he died, in Boston playing with Larry Coryell. A couple of nights before he went to Boston, he came to my apartment and borrowed a bass.

It's undoubtedly a difficult thing to preserve your talent. It's something that requires a sense of daily vigilance. They're all kinds of ways you can screw up. You can screw up by simply not practicing enough. Or you can screw up by messing up your life to the point where you can't play well. A lucky few manage to skate through. I do think there are some people who I've known that have knowingly shortened their life and lived hard and brilliantly, at least in part because they felt they were being true to their gift.

Their best course was to get everything out they could in a limited period of time.

The Road to Damascus

The first recording I made, which happened a few months after I arrived in New York, was with the Jimmy Giuffre 3, *Free Fall*. Jimmy had a multi-album contract with Verve, and had given them, over a period of a few years, some recordings that were successful for them, notably *The Train and the River*. His trios had produced a kind of amiable folksy music that Verve was happy to record and distribute. The trio with Jim Hall and Ralph Peña, which I love dearly: that was wonderful music.

Then Jimmy had a "Road to Damascus" experience when he heard Ornette Coleman and all of a sudden started playing free. He hired Paul Bley to abet him in this. and Paul brought me into the band. We showed up at a New York recording studio for the new Jimmy Giuffre 3 recording playing free music. It was something close to revolutionary for its time. Creed Taylor was producing the record date. The irony is that it sounds amiable now. It's no longer threatening — at least to me. It's just three guys trying to play some music. We were grouping towards consonance and all that.

I had the same impression of Ornette's music. When I first heard Ornette at the Five Spot, it was a shock, a physical shock. I was reeling from what he was doing. When I return to the music he made at that time now, it's warm, welcoming, inviting, and not in the least an assault. At the time, Ornette didn't perceive it that way. He was just playing the music that he loved to play. There was not the intention to turn the world on its head. The world got turned on its head as a byproduct of what they were doing.

My Hands Were Saying

The change to electric bass was something that happened to me, not something that I did. I was playing with Gary Burton in the late 1960s. He and I had a gig at what was the precursor to the NAMM Show. Musser Marimbas was paying Gary, and Gary was paying me to work with him, twenty minutes on, forty minutes off, at this show, which included every known musical instrument manufacturer at the time.

We did it for two or three days, and I got incredibly restless after the first few hours of this. I'd gone around to every booth but the electric, because I had the typical jazz musician prejudice against this instrument. At a certain point there was nothing left to do, and I felt like I was skulking into a dirty movie. I loitered around the Gibson booth and waited until I was sure nobody saw me and then slipped in. I touched an electric bass and fell in love. My immediate response was my brain saying, "No, don't do this." My hands were saying, "I love the feel of this instrument." It was a quandary that I had been put into.

I loved this instrument that was not at all well regarded in the jazz community. What was I supposed to do? I had no desire to change my vocabulary to become a rock and roll musician or a rhythm and blues musician. I wanted to continue exactly what I was doing, but I wanted to do it on the electric bass. There was something irresistible about the feel and response of the instrument that resonated with me. That's been something of a lifetime issue: how to play the electric bass in a jazz context and how to convince other jazz musicians to bend sufficiently to become comfortable playing with the electric bass. It's been a fascinating and ongoing challenge to bring the electric bass into areas it's not generally been in, in the past.

My Heart and Little Else

I had been playing The Trident for weeks on end when I was with Gary Burton, and I developed an infatuation with Marin County. When I wanted to leave New York, the place that most appealed to me was Marin County. I just went out there with hope in my heart and little else, and found my way into a music scene.

I connected with Lowell Levinger, "Banana," when I moved to Marin County in 1970. I moved to a legendary town called Bolinas. It was full of poets: Robert Creeley, Lawrence Ferlinghetti, Joanne

Kyger. Gary Snyder was coming through all the time. It was an incredibly vital scene to be living in.

I was right down the coast where Banana and Joe Bauer the drummer lived. They were two-thirds of The Youngbloods. We cut an album together. I met them through my bass-playing friend Jack Gregg. He was friends from his youth with Joe Bauer, who came from Memphis.

I got to hang out with Jefferson Airplane and go to lots of Grateful Dead concerts. I was also playing with Art Lande and Mike Nock, so there was also a jazz scene and a very fluid movement back and forth between various scenes. Eliot Zigmund was the drummer at the time.

A Bad Rap?

The drummers are, in my opinion, the intellectuals in the music. This runs contrary to the stereotype of the drummer as sort of a "noble savage." Point in fact, the drummers are the mathematicians on the bandstand.

Pete La Roca and I found each other when it was easy to break rules. It was easy to go as far out on a limb as you chose to go. There was an atmosphere on the bandstand that not only encouraged that but demanded it. The infection was not contained in the rhythm section—the horn players were feeling it, too. They were eager for the kind of surprises and sense of uncertainty that hadn't been there a few years before. Guys like Blue Mitchell and Junior Cook, who are two of my very favorite players, wanted that reassurance from Gene Taylor. The way they played wanted that.

As Long As There Are Women

It's mysterious to me that the blues resonated so deeply in my life, because I was a white suburban kid in a entirely white New Jersey suburban community. When I heard the blues, it hit me right between the eyes. I was the only kid in my town who was affected in that way. I've come to realize there's probably one kid in every suburban town that somehow was hit just as hard by what's in the blues and what's in jazz, which is a deep strain of the blues. When I listen to Charlie Parker I hear the same kind of blues that I hear when I listen to B. B. King. It's present in Coltrane as well and it's not going to go away. There may be a dilution of that impulse in the music that's coming out of the schools, but the blues is in no danger of going away. As long as there are women to break your heart, there's going to be the blues.

BILLY COBHAM

The drummer Billy Cobham grew up in an age before interconnectivity. His art reflects selflessness, camaraderie, and freedom of expression, which are the same values I want to promote for my two young daughters and future generations of curious human beings. There has been no segregation in his music or the musicians, be it Horace Silver, dreaming with the Brecker brothers, atmospheric sounds with Jan Hammer and Jeremy Steig, finding Snoopy with Leland Sklar and Tommy Bolin, or developing the dynamic rhythm sections in the studio and out. Then there have been the unrelenting tours with George Duke and John Abercrombie, NAMM show jams with Steve Miller, Brazilian Swing with Astrud Gilberto, Grover Washington Jr., Bobby and the Midnites, Freddie Hubbard, John McLaughlin, Milt Jackson, and Carlos Santana.

Billy's focus has always remained the same: communicate without using his voice and be himself. Woodshed for hours and leave it all on the stage.

I have interviewed Billy five times on my radio show: in September 2013, June 2014, April 2015, April 2017, and April 2019. In these interviews we talk about the genius of Miles Davis in the studio, leaving your physical body on the bandstand, the conception and realization of Mahavishnu Orchestra, and the primary role of a drummer.

The Real Leader

Contrary to popular belief, the leader of the band is the guy who plays the drums. They don't want to accept that, but it's true. You let the band not play without a drummer and see what kind of problems they have. If they don't have a drummer, everybody goes off on their own and they decide that they're going to lead by playing louder, faster, and for as long as they want. Pretty soon no one is listening to each other.

If there's a good solid player who lays it down and is consistent and can make you feel comfortable at what you do, you become dependent on them in less than 30 seconds because you know someone's got your back. That's when the drums and the drummer come forward.

When there's a problem, everybody looks back and says "Hey, what's wrong?" It may be them, but they're looking at the person in the back. That's the person they're expecting to support them.

You About You

The priority is to keep the tempo and play a solo within it. I was told by a few musicians, "Don't worry, man, I'm not going to sound bad. I'm going to play my ass off." I'm thinking, "What about the rest of the band? What are we going to do when you're playing your ass off? Especially if it has nothing to do with what we're doing. Why do we need you?"

It's about the band effort, and if that in fact is true and we're all following that particular dogma, then it should be right there, all the time, every time. When all that other stuff is happening, and you're not doing "this," it's criminal, because it means you're only thinking for you. Don't go there....

If you're playing with a band, you have to be thinking for the band. The band is all-encompassing and most important. You lay it down for the band and the band will help you. The best compliment you can get is that "the band sounded good." As soon as someone tells you about you, you got a problem.

I Can Only Do This

Horace Silver was a role model for me. He didn't do everything you wanted him to. He couldn't be good for everybody: he had to be good to Horace first. Horace also had a family; he was out there busting his butt for them. The one thing that I realized, he only had so much. He'd say, "Man I can only do this. If you can do better, God bless. Don't worry, you go ahead and do that. I'll work it out, I'll find somebody."

I respected that greatly, and I carry that ethos in me to this day. I can't be everything to everybody else. I gotta do what I have to do. I've got to stand by my points and feelings. Try to do the best I can for the people who are with me, in the best way.

That said, Horace was super-organized. From getting all the music together to writing everything, having everybody feeling very comfortable. He knew what kind of personality he wanted to have presented as a group. He was not a cheap man; he had quality. He didn't have the budget, and that was very, very special. He's saying, "This is all I can do. So we have to work within these parameters here. I want to get the most out of everybody including myself." We get up on the bandstand and because he's so organized, we would play our butts off. The music was just swinging. From the very first note there was something there to grasp.

We played six nights for two weeks, three weeks. Those were the days when a band could have a concert date and somehow stay in one place for a long period of time. You can't do that now. Most bands don't have a chance to be together that long. From 1975 to the present, generally speaking, musicians have all been competing with each other.

The 25-Minute Accident

Jack DeJohnette introduced me to Miles Davis. I ended up starting to work in the studio with Miles, and what I learned from those experiences was that Miles was an artistic director. He knew how to match up a player to the music.

When he called you for a project, he already knew what you were going to play. He knew that what was there would be perfectly set for you. So you knew it was going to be in your wheelhouse and you were thinking, "This is going to be fun."

Hence things like *Jack Johnson*. It wasn't supposed to happen; it was an accident. It was a 25-minute accident. I can't even remember what we rehearsed, because Miles said in the studio when we got there, "Remember what you played last night?" I was so petrified that I lied and said "OK." He answered, "Show me." So I played and he said, "That's not what you played last night. But I like that—play that!"

Present in Me

On Miles's *Bitches Brew* and *Jack Johnson*, I had an advantage. It was the guy with the trumpet pointing at people. His aura was that strong that you knew when to play and when not to play. What was special about Miles was that I could add that aura to my musical palette. Take direction from him in body language, so to speak. Contribute where I felt it was necessary.

We would only play what we thought was necessary to give the music life. It wasn't about how many notes we played, or how advanced we were on our instruments, individually. It was about the real picture that was put forward and how that personality would be instilled in the minds that would listen.

When you left the studio and the record came out, people would know all the lines exactly. I knew the guys on the sessions from reputation, but I had never played with any of them. I found the first thing I needed to do was "not" play. Show restraint. Not because I couldn't, but because I wanted to understand the direction in which the music was going.

Miles was a very special person. I say "was"— is, because he's still very present in me and I believe in many of my contemporaries.

On Breathing

What John McLaughlin and I started in 1970 was so spontaneous. We were down in an old apartment in Soho. John and I first met on a record date that Quincy Jones put together for a Sean Connery soundtrack titled *The Anderson Tapes*. He had four guitar players: McLaughlin, Herb Ellis, Eric Gale, and Jim Hall. Those were the four guitar players.

I took Grady Tate's place. Grady was busy doing something else; he couldn't finish the record, so I subbed for him. Hank Jones was on piano, George Duvivier on bass. Just some silly big band! I think even Leon Pendarvis was in on it.

We used to do this earlier on when we had some tunes and time. In fact, I still have my quarter-inch tapes. We'd get together and jam with Chick Corea and Joe Zawinul, Wayne Shorter, maybe even Larry Coryell, Miroslav Vitous. Just sitting in somebody else's house with a 12-track Scully machine, just because.

The conversation went something like this:

"What are you doing?"

"Oh, I'm at home, having a coffee."

"Why don't you come over and bring your drums? I want to try out of couple of tunes."

I would just go. I was living in the Village. Most of us were, so we would walk. I mean I didn't have anything else to do, and we had such respect for each other. It didn't take much to get people out of the house, meet somewhere and play. With that came the camaraderie of John and me. So when he asked me to come play, I said, "OK."

We would start out playing around 10 in the morning; we'd have a couple of sandwiches for lunch. We'd play till 5 o'clock in the afternoon and wouldn't even know the sun had gone down.

Two things popped up for me. I was not strong playing odd meters, and I wanted to get command of that. I was also playing a lot of notes and not controlling my breathing. I was really working on this, and John lent me a hand because he was really into yoga at that time. I started to understand yoga breathing, which is fundamentally playing within yourself; playing every note of the music in the same way you would have an everyday conversation with a best friend. So you're emotional, of course, but you never stop breathing! You present everything in an emotional way, and that's the way it is.

One day led to the next, and after ten days John says, "I want to try this band." I never turn anything down, and it wasn't like work was coming in like crazy. I mean if they want you to play "Beer Barrel Polka" you play "Beer Barrel Polka" until they say, "That's not 'Beer Barrel Polka,'" and then you're fired.

The next thing you know we are in, and it was a natural transition. Next thing, John says, "I want to bring in this piano player." I said "Who?" He says, "I want to get Jan Hammer. He's playing with Sarah Vaughan right now and he sounds really good." Then he wanted to bring in this violinist who I had not heard much about, so I had to do my homework. Turns out it was Jerry Goodman. He plays a lot of notes, and I'm trying to figure out why. At the same time, he's got this incredible tone that synchronized really well with John. You can hear this on *My Goal's Beyond*.

At that point I said, "Now I understand, now I understand." We also had an anchor: his name was Charlie Haden. And the music was blossoming when our true anchor, Rick Laird, came along a few months later.

Watching from Above

Mahavishnu Orchestra was playing at The Olympia in Paris and we were very tired. We had been on the road maybe eight or ten weeks between the United States and Europe. No real time off, away from each other. We were just hittin' it, because the iron was very hot and we had to strike.

We finally got to the last date before a two-week break. The next thing you know, I'm tired and we're playing, and it's now about 2½ hours into the show. Normally we play about a 3-, 3½-hour show. It's one song after the next, one song after the next. I might only play a little on a ballad like "Lotus."

We were so synchronized. This is what happens when you're so in tune with the music and the individuals playing it. Much of what happens becomes automatic. Your subconscious clicks in to a point where it's running the body on automatic. It's like running a plane on automatic. And all of a sudden, the brain goes into a second mode and you can literally go away from it, and like a ghost you can watch everybody.

I remember being on the bandstand and watching myself partially fall asleep on the snare drum as we were playing, because

I was tired. I saw everything happening around me and I also realized we needed to start closing this down because we needed to catch a flight.

All this stuff is going on and I'm thinking about managing the band and what we need to do. "Where's Elliott?" the road manager. "What's he doing?" And we're playing to something like 1,500 to 2,000 people, jammed. It might have been the second show that afternoon, I don't know.

We were just in a zone and everything was working. It all seemed so comfortable. And when it was time to come out of this tune, we came out and went right in to "Awakening," and that's when I woke up. We started playing and I was right there, but I could remember everything that happened before then and I wasn't on the bandstand. I was physically there, everything was moving, everything was working, but I watched that whole part of the show from outside of myself.

The Art of Three

The late Toots Thielemans got a call in 2013 from somebody who wanted him to play in Italy. He forgot that he had already made a commitment to never leave Belgium again. He was going to stay in Brussels, and that's the only place he was going.

The promoter received the money. Months went by and now it was time to get to work. Somebody called Toots and said, "We have a gig in Italy." He said, "No, we don't. I'm retired." They said, "Well, you agreed to do this months ago." He said, "Give the sponsors the money back." He canceled the date, God bless him.

I got a call from the promoter asking if I could put a band together on a couple of days' notice. I have this project with Ron Carter and Kenny Barron from time to time; it doesn't happen very often. It's the perfect stop-gap band-aid, if you need a band real quick. Why? Because what I learned with Ron and Kenny, with Jimmy Owens and Larry Willis—we learned repertoire.

There are so few musicians who know repertoire nowadays. What repertoire means is that you can call between 100 and 250 different tunes at any time or any tempo (that makes sense), in any key within reason, and play those tunes on a gig without having to rehearse. We took the gig and had a ball.

Bird Lives

The world has become a lot smaller because of traveling. That means that many of the personalities in this country have been able to go forth, outside the shores, and spread the musical word throughout the world. It's become a common thing to have people play together who come from all different parts of the world.

Take a tune like Ron Carter's "81," and hearing somebody from India play that tune. The pianist and bass player are from Turkey, in the same band. You have all these combinations of people playing "81." When you hear it, you go, "Really?" Yea, it'll work.

The funny thing is, you turn around and say, "You're into those sessions?" They go, "Yeah, we studied at Berklee." That's when I run the other way. It's amazing how many people have said that to me, from Thailand, Singapore, Malaysia, Indonesia, China: everybody studied at Berklee and they know all these tunes.

I was in Budapest and I went to the local football stadium for a percussion festival. The opening act was The Mongolian String Jazz Quartet. They were playing "Scrapple from the Apple." They were playing these bowed string instruments and another guy was throat singing. The drummer had all these tablas and a bass drum. It worked. I thought, "Wow, Charlie Parker made it to the steppes of Mongolia."

See also Brian K. Gruber, *Six Days at Ronnie Scott's: Billy Cobham on Jazz Fusion and the Act of Creation* (Create Space, 2018).

DAVID LINDLEY

David Lindley is a multi-instrumentalist who has command of instruments from around the world. Lindley plays primarily string instruments, including the acoustic and electric guitar, upright and electric bass, banjo, lap steel guitar, mandolin, hardingfele, bouzouki, cittern, bağlama, gumbus, charango, cümbüş, oud, and zither.

He has used them in a variety of musical settings over the years as both a studio musician and on the bandstand. He was part of the avant-garde psychedelic folk-rock ensemble Kaleidoscope. He has collaborated and recorded with Terry Reid, Jackson Browne, David Crosby and Graham Nash, Warren Zevon, and Ben Harper, and on *El Rayo-X*.

I have interviewed David four times on my radio show between October 2017 and August 2019. Our discussions have included the origins of punk music, the hotbed of folk music that was Southern California, starting his career as a banjo teacher, and how technology has changed authenticity in music.

Bear Branch

The significance of music in our culture has changed on a lot of fronts. The folk music now, they kind of think it's one thing in particular — the Americana kind of stuff. Folk-music-sounding folk music.

The real serious folk music is hip hop, gangster rap, all that. It comes from people who are making it up out of their heads. You didn't attend any class for it. It's a totally different approach, and really relevant to everybody's life where these guys live.

Songs that Woody Guthrie wrote: it's the same intensity; it's with the same passion and intent. It's like the folk musicians in Turkey. One guy gets ahold of an oud and starts playing stuff on there, and he gets really, really good. He doesn't study any of the classical stuff: he just plays it like a folk instrument. He gets really good, so he develops this one style. Somebody over in Iran does the same thing with a tar, which is like a Persian banjo. Down the road a little bit in Azerbaijan they play a completely different style and you ask them how and they say, "Well, we just got together. We play this stuff now and it becomes a regional style."

You had this happening all over the U.S. at one time. We'd borrow from Buzzy down the road, but then we'd hear about this great fiddle player from Kentucky. We'd have to look him up. Everybody knows where he is: "Just go to the post office in Bear Branch and ask where Nate is." Two fiddle players would go along on the trip and they'd come back and they'd start playing like this guy.

Sit on a Stool

I went to see Charles Mingus at The Dragonwyk Club in Pasadena, and it was just world-changing. At one point I was thinking, "I want to do that." It was his overall presence, and the stuff he played that seemed to be impossible, and the sound he got. He was kind of an animal. I wanted to do what Mingus did, the upright bass.

When I was a little kid, they wanted someone to play the upright bass in the school orchestra and they asked me to step up and try it. I was kinda of small, but I was really strong, so I could play it. The first time I got my hands on it, I said, "I know what this is, I can play this." They answered, "Well, you're too small for this. You have to be a little bigger." I said, "Well, I can sit on a stool." I started playing it like a jazz player. I was about 10 or 12 years old.

The First Bouzouki

I was a fan of classical Indian music from my dad's record collection. He had Yehudi Menuhin records. He bought Ravi Shankar's first album on World Pacific, *Ragas & Talas*. My dad was very hip about all kinds of stuff. He would listen to stuff that was really pretty serious. He was a corporation lawyer for 20th Century Fox. He played piano and loved different kinds of music from all over the world.

The first bouzouki playing I ever heard was a soundtrack to some film. He loved the film because of the traditional Greek music, *Rembetika*. I had never heard anything like that. I asked him, "What is that instrument?" He said, "It's kind of like a mandolin with a long neck." There was a picture of it, and I noted, "Oh, one of those."

The wheels started turning, and there were some great players in those days, too. Because of that, I went into playing different kinds of folk music. Playing bluegrass, I had been listening to Earl Scruggs and Don Reno. I had also been listening to Sabicas, the Flamenco guitarist.

Hillbilly

Jim Keltner and I shared a studio for a while at Berry and Grassmueck Music. I'd get a Coke from the Coke machine and I'd put it on his snare drum. One day I spilled Coke into this priceless old Ludwig. He got really pissed off.

The snare drum was prominent. There were other drums in there, too, but the snare drum was being used for rudiments and marching.

Keltner used to work behind the counter downstairs and sell stuff every once in a while. I never got to do that. Management kind of had this idea about me, "He's not a real guy, he's a folk musician," which was not a bona fide musician. "Oh, he plays five-string banjo: that's hillbilly music."

Cat's Pajamas

Ed Pearl, who was the owner of the Ash Grove in Los Angeles, would have people come in. He would make sure these Mississippi sharecroppers had the transportation, had a place to stay, and he paid them really well to come to The Ash Grove and play for a week. We all went there and we'd hear these guys play and go, "Holy sh**!" It was all people of a certain age: me, Ry Cooder, Al Marian, Sandy Mosley, David Cohen, we'd learn all this stuff and we had our version of it.

Jim Kweskin was the resident guru at The Cat's Pajamas in Arcadia, where I played all the time. That was the first time I heard Kweskin. He was getting together a jug band and he was looking around for people in East LA. There were a lot of fantastic players there.

I used to go see Mike McClellan every time he played. He played the twelve-string like Leadbelly, he played the banjo like Ralph Stanley, and he sang. I'd go see him all the time.

It was the folk process. You didn't go to school, you went to the club. You absorbed and you learned how to steal.

We Came to the Conclusion

In those days, mid–late 1960s, there was free-form radio, Tom Donahue. You would hear George Jones, Ravi Shankar, and Jean-Luc Ponty, and then some more George Jones. It was that way on purpose, which was a statement, a really eloquent statement, which is: "Music is pretty much the same, for the same reasons." It showed everybody that all these people were going through pretty much the same thing. It's all valid.

Anything that sounded good to me, I would go after. I heard Sabicas play Flamenco, and that was a huge moment. I said, "I want to do that. I'll try some of that out." Then I realized I would have needed to start out when I was 17 years old to learn all that complex traditional Flamenco.

I was listening to Ravi Shankar and classical North Indian music. I loved all that stuff. It was during that period that The Beatles came out of 'all of that stuff.' To me they sounded like folkies except plugged in. "I Want to Hold Your Hand" is like The Louvin Brothers, Jim & Jesse, and The Virginia Boys. It all sounded so familiar. It's OK to plug in. That's what happened.

Jerry Garcia and I had a conversation about this one time, and we came to the conclusion that it was pretty much the same thing. He approached The Grateful Dead stuff as a bluegrass musician. That approach was familiar to me, 'cause that's the one I use, plus a bunch of other stuff.

On My Way

There were a couple of banjo players I really loved. One was Billy Faier, who played all kinds of classical banjo stuff. I heard him, and then I heard Marshall Brickman. He played this really unusual style that I'd never seen before. There was also Tom Paley of the New Lost City Ramblers who played with his fingernails—it was more interesting. That whole thing about style over content. Some people go for the style over the content.

There's much more content in "ethnic folk music." I could also get down and dirty with all the real deep Appalachian Smokey Mountain banjo stuff and Ozark Music of the fiddle: hillbilly music. That fascinated me, and you would get this feeling. I learned to recognize it because at the same time I was also interested in Flamenco guitar, which did the same thing to me. I said, "Well, they're pretty close." What is it about these things, different styles from completely different areas, what is it about this that I like? It was the same thing. I started listening to all kinds of music.

Sandy Bull was around playing the oud. Hamza El Din. I started listening to everything. When I would go on the road with Jackson Browne, I would have three Alan Stivell (Breton harp) cassettes and *Shantung—Music of Confucius' Homeland*. I would play those on the road when I'd go to my hotel room. Stivell was a monster; he was a huge folk figurehead in France and all over Europe. He was unbelievably influential. He could really sing and play that old-style harp. After that I was on my way....

Factions

Kaleidoscope played a lot of stuff where we'd have a theme, then elaborate on the theme. Chester Crill, the fiddle and harmonica player, listened to jazz all the time. He would bring a lot of that into Kaleidoscope. We played "Straight No Chaser." Then we would play a Balkan thing in 7/8 or 5/8.

Solomon Feldthouse would take a saw solo with all the quarter tones; people really didn't know what to do. We just kept playing what interested us. It was an experiment and it worked for a long time until there were different factions within the Kaleidoscope group. There was the RnB and Blues faction and the Middle Eastern/Balkan faction. That was bound to happen one way or another. The record company didn't know what to do with us because we didn't fall into any category.

Drum Solos

There was a gig we did with Don Ellis at The Aquarius Theatre. He was really encouraging to us. He said, "Do what you want, play what you like, don't try to sell records. Play what you like, and people will recognize what's good."

I asked Jim Keltner if he would play with Kaleidoscope. He said, "Well, I can't 'cause I got all these gigs I got to do." He recommended Paul Lagos, who was a jazz drummer. He was a killer player and added a lot of stuff. When he would do drum solos, they were real drum solos, really dynamic.

Paul was from Hell's Kitchen, but when he moved out to LA he had a house in Mt. Washington. He was a health-food freak; he raised his own food and had goats. He also shot heroin. "Paul, have you ever considered that there's a conflict here?" He said, "Yes, I've often thought of that. It bothers me a lot, but I'll get through it."

He was the first person who knew who George Gurdjieff, the Armenian philosopher, was. Gurdjieff developed his own "Fourth Way" of waking people up.

Watching a Shaman

I was upstairs in the dressing room at Family Dog at The Great Highway, which was essentially The Avalon II in San Francisco. Charlie Musselwhite was on stage, and I didn't know who the people in his band were. This insane sax player started taking the solo and I said, "I got to see this. This is really good. What weird stuff!"

Me and Solomon came running down the stairs, stood by the side of the stage, and jumped up and down. It was not a sax, it was a lap steel guitar: Freddie Roulette sitting in his chair with a pipe in his mouth. He had on a pink-and-black V-neck Cardigan sweater. He was very neat; he wasn't a hippy like we were. It was the real thing, and it was totally original as far as the kind of stuff that he was playing with Charlie. He knew all the Alvino Rey, all these great Hawaiian guitar players. He learned how to play stuff that no one else could play.

He could play "Holiday for Strings" with all the passing chords and he would slap the bar to get all these different intervals. In watching him, it was like watching a shaman raise another dimension from the earth. To this day I have never seen anything like that.

Freddie would do these runs every once in a while. He would tune the steel guitar in such a way that he could get these scales and inflections that I had never heard. Especially rock and roll players, they didn't do that. Country and Western players at the time were mostly pedal steel.

Are You Using Your Thumb?

When the San Fernando earthquake hit in 1971, we were stuck in London in a hotel room. Sugarcane Harris was there, and the only thing to do while we were listening to the radio to see if Los Angeles was rubble was listen to Sugarcane play. He played this fiddle stuff, and I watched what he played. As a fiddle player, I figured out a lot of what that was. How to play the false harmonics in "Soul Motion." He showed me what it was. He said, "This is how you do this. Don't press all the way down, you're pressing down too hard. Just like that." Every once in while I got to run into guys like that and I would ask them questions, "Why do you do this? How do you do that? Are you using your thumb? How far does your thumb go over?" I took it all in....

Time to Write Songs

Punk music's evolution was part of the cyclical nature of music. You had people neatly packaged and promoted and managed, doing all the stuff the big machine wanted. The punk movement went so far as to say, "We're not going to learn to play too well. Fuck you guys, and we got something to say. Here it is—you better listen." It was another scene, too, because LA was just insanity. Dead Kennedys and Black Flag and all these places where people went.

It was an alternative to what they viewed as "corporate rock." It was a structure that you became part of. If a record company was interested in you, they would sign you, and you would become part of their roster of artists, and you would release albums on their label. Then you'd have a manager who would coordinate all the stuff, and the manager and the record company would coordinate promotional things.

The artist and the manager would take advantage of everything the record company was able to do for them. Then you'd go out and play these gigs and make a video. In those days, that was a big thing, too. The record company would take certain things out of the picture that you didn't have to worry about anymore. You didn't have to self-promote; they handled that. You didn't have to go around and play open mics, because everything would be organized. You had your manager, the booking agent, and the record company, and they all worked together. One of the reasons that that particular structure worked was that you had time to write songs.

The punk movement wasn't a cold-hearted participation in the corporate entity. A lot of my friends who were in the punk scene wrote songs. They were prolific song writers and they'd go and just play some place. That's what I did, too; I did everything. It was very well timed because I was right in the middle of it. All these opportunities where you turn around and something's happening that you could do if you wanted to.

The Cher Box

The advent of the pitch corrector for vocals is a huge thing. You may not be a good singer, and it's really hard to get a vocal that goes all the way through that's in tune and it's really good.

You put it through "the box." For a while, it was called "The Cher Box" because she really used it a lot and actually used it like an instrument and messed with the repeat. She got some pretty interesting stuff out of it.

The basic purpose of the box was to get perfect vocals, or take other instruments and tune those things up. Light bulbs went off in the heads of producers and record companies. "We'll get somebody who has charisma of some sort, and we'll make it that they sound really good."

In country music 99.9% of all vocals are run through a DigiTech. There's all kinds of different models of that thing, and they use it. You can't tell the difference a lot of the time.

There was an expression in the 1970s, "Beware of those without instruments." Can they really play or is it just a façade and you trying to get away with something? It's like the boy bands that didn't play, that was it.

DAVID GARIBALDI

David Garibaldi developed his own rhythm on the drum kit. He merged a sophisticated big-band swing feel with the indigenous funk rhythms of Bernard Purdie, Clyde Stubblefield, and Jabo Starks. His style was also enhanced by all the drummers around him in Oakland and San Francisco: guys like Sandy McKee, Gaylord Birch, and Michael Shrieve.

Garibaldi has been the driving force behind the band Tower of Power since their inception over fifty ago, being able to play live for nights at a time behind singers like Lenny Williams and Rick Stevens, or holding down while Doc Kupka and Emilio Castillo blew over the top.

He has the chops to play in any musical setting, because he can feel the cats around him and is always listening to them.

I have interviewed David three times on my radio program: December 2013, September 2014, and December 2016. We also did a Facebook Live Interview at the Musical Instrument Museum in Phoenix in December 2017. In these excepts we discuss the evolution of American military music and bands, the drum games he would play with other Bay Area drummers, showing respect to mentors who came before us, and how he joined Tower of Power.

That Was Vulgar
I remember when I was playing with Mickey Hart, Zakir Hussain was in the band. One day he came to the gig and he handed all of us incense. He said, "Today is the day in India that we pay tribute to our teachers. Whoever it is who taught you, today's the day you pay tribute to them."

In modern society are we taught to have a special day to think about the lessons we've learned from our teachers? I don't think so. To me that was such an awesome thing that he would want to include me in that. I never forgot it, because it's really important. This is real, this is what you do, this is how you learn, this is how you pass on what you're doing.

I got out of high school, I was 17 years old. I had been playing on Tuesday nights with the Sid Reece Big Band in Livermore, CA on the back of a flatbed truck outside of his music store.

They were all older guys. I don't know why they liked the way I played, 'cause I didn't have anything together yet. I couldn't even play an 8-bar solo. I can hardly do it now! They taught me a lot of stuff. It was the first time I discovered I could actually make money doing this.

They got me a New Year's Eve gig with a stripper. I had never seen anything like that before. I had only one stick and one brush. I somehow forgot to get all my gear together. They were really upset about that, especially the stripper. I couldn't hit her moves. With a stick and a brush, it was like "boom, swish."

The first money I made playing music was big band jazz. I always loved that kind of music, and I love jazz music. When I was coming up, that's how you had credibility—if you were a jazz musician. Being a rock musician, that was vulgar. It wasn't anything, and certainly not what it became.

When I joined Tower, and the years right before I joined Tower, I decided to play funk and RnB but use all the things I was learning from other genres and fuse them together. That was at the cusp of when that was happening. Guys were making decisions about where they were going to go musically. For me, I wanted to fuse things together. All the guys that I played with, that's what we did.

Study with Me

I came up on the cusp of the rock and roll era. Learning was very different than it has become. You had to get the records; you had listen to what guys did. You had to try to figure out what they were doing from the records.

Maybe if you were lucky you'd get to see them if they came through your town. So it was difficult to build a playing personality. You could do it, but the end result was very individual sounding players, because there wasn't all this stuff to copy. You had to figure it out for yourself.

There were standard jazz tunes that everybody had to know. You learned to play those things and then you'd go out and play with people. Everybody played the same kind of tunes and it's not like that now.

What I tell people if they want to study with me is that I do things in a very personal sort of way. I developed my own way to play, based on all the things I was hearing. I put together my vocabulary doing that, copying guys. I never did much transcribing, not till later. Transcribing is a good way understand *what* people are playing. Ultimately you have to take the things that you're learning and you have to do your thing with them, because this is art, no more no less. It's an expression of what you see in the music that you want to play. That takes a lot of time; it takes a lot of playing sessions. So that's what I encourage my students to do.

Military Music

Military music, at the time that I was in, was not modern by any stretch of the imagination. It was marching bands. We had a symphonic band that was really amazingly good. We had small combos, we had a jazz group.

So the young guys were bringing in music to play. The older guys didn't dig it, because they were rooted in military music tradition, which was Glen Miller marches, John Philip Sousa marches. During that time I was in, all these young people were coming in during Vietnam. They were changing the way that military music was being played, because it was young people coming in with all these new influences. It was a big change for military music. I liked the military and I considered staying in, but the music thing sucked; it was going nowhere. Then they changed it, so it was more contemporary.

I was in a field band. In the military, the bands you want to be in were the headquarters bands. There was the NORAD Band out of Colorado Springs. It was a combination of bands, including Canadian.

There was a band in Omaha, Nebraska at the SAC headquarters;

they had a pretty serious band there. The other bands you wanted to be in were the bands in DC. All the bands, The Air Force Band, The Marine Band, The Army Band, The Coast Guard Band, were the cream of the crop. If I had stayed in the military, I would have tried to get in one of those.

Best Thing I Ever Did

When you're 23 years old, ignorance is bliss. I wanted to be in a band with horns. I wanted to play funky music. I wanted to express myself musically. I wasn't really interested in anything else. I didn't even think about how I was going to make a living. I just wanted to play music. My whole thing was that. I just wanted to be in a band and that's what I did. I got to join Tower of Power and it was the best thing I ever did.

One of the first gigs with Tower of Power we stayed in a van with our gear and slept on the floors of clubs. I didn't care. Looking back at it now, I'm saying, "Gosh I did that?" At the time it was no big deal. We've always been in it together. Our music is about working together. Drummers and bass players, for instance: we never talk about what we do together; we just do it. I think that's important working together.

Like a Rainbow

There were a bunch of different guys: Bill Vitt, Gaylord Birch, Mike Clark. Harvey Hughes was an absolutely killer drummer. Greg Errico is a very good friend; he was one of my heroes with Sly and the Family Stone. Willie Sparks, who was with Graham Central Station. Sam Cox was another great drummer in Oakland. Sandy McKee with Cold Blood. Everybody had their own vibe—it was the "Oakland sound."

The music scene in The Bay Area has always been integrated. Always people of color mixing; it was like a rainbow. Everybody was always working together. That's what I remember when I was coming up. There were never any sort of racial issues. There definitely were in other parts of society, but as far as musicians, it was a place that was safe for everyone. You could come and enjoy each other and share ideas. It was really, really cool. I remember there were a lot of places to play, and that's how music was made. You played in the clubs and you took what was available. There wasn't a big road scene; it was all regional. Guys would come to each other's gigs.

That's the way everybody did it in those days. The thing that is different from then versus today is that there weren't all these media to look at. There wasn't YouTube, there wasn't video. There was only records and audio tapes, so the only way you learned how to play was by listening to the recordings. Maybe you'd catch your favorite drummer if he was coming through town. You were left to your own devices. "What is this dude doing here? What's he up to?" You didn't get to see them play, so you had to use your imagination. Eventually it turned into your own personal statement.

We went and watched the guys that we liked. We watched all our friends play and then we'd hang out. Harvey Hughes and I used to get together at my place in Oakland and just play all day. We'd exchange ideas. One guy would sit at the drum set and the other would say, "Why don't you move your hand over here. Why don't you try this, why don't you try that." We'd tag-team on the drum set all day and give each other little challenges. We came up with some of the most nasty, cool-sounding grooves and beats. It was a collective mind that was going on, everybody wanted to be their own person.

The Reality Sandwich

I remember when I first came back from the military, it was 1969 and I started working around the Bay Area, and two of the first people I met were Mike Clark and Paul Jackson. They were already a team. Mike was a really accomplished player even in those days. He was already a great jazz drummer when I met him. He could do all the funk and the other stuff, but his jazz thing was really outstanding.

Paul, when I met him, he had this little sweater on with elbow patches—this really nerdy short dude. But those guys were really, really cool, and Mike and I used to be in this band together. We shared the drum chair in a band called The Reality Sandwich, which was an East Bay sort of a deal. We used to play at this club called On Broadway in Jack London Square. Every Tuesday night there we had a gig: a regular in-town gig where everybody used to come and hang and jam.

That's where I met the Tower of Power guys. Skip Mesquite and Mic Gillette were Tower guys who used to come sit in with The Reality Sandwich band. One night they asked me if I wanted to come check out their band. I had never heard of them, but the minute I heard them, I realized it was the only music I wanted to play.

In the first year and a half when I joined TOP, every Monday and Tuesday night we used to play at On Broadway. After the gig, we would hang out all night listening to the radio. We would sit there and just groove; party and hang out together. We would sit there and listen to music, and then we would dream about what we wanted our band to be.

Frenchy's was a really fancy supper club that became more of a rock and roll kind of place where everybody started playing. There was one night we had a jam there and all these people came: Stevie Wonder was in there, Redbone, Cold Blood, and they're all lined up in there ready to jam.

Get a New Drummer

Tower of Power got their record deal on a Tuesday night gig at The Fillmore that was called Sounds of the City. It was a battle-of-the-bands kind of thing. They were on the verge of breaking up—this was about a year or so before I joined them.

One of the prizes was a record deal with one of Bill Graham's labels. He had San Francisco Records and Fillmore Records. One was distributed by Columbia and one distributed by Atlantic. The band won this record deal, and the producer they were signed to,

David Rubinson, told them, "Your drummer's got to get it together. We'll give it six months. But if nothing changes, you're going to have to go get a new drummer if you want to record." The drummer was Emilio Castillo's brother Jack. It was tough for Emilio to fire his brother.

The band was assigned to Bill Graham's label, San Francisco Records, which was distributed by Atlantic. I joined the band on July 23rd 1970. I knew I was going to be in the band from the first time I heard them. I knew I was going to be in it before I knew anybody. It had "me" written all over it. It was everything I wanted in music when I heard them.

We recorded in September and that was a live recording. *East Bay Grease* was a live recording with a few little overdubs. We released it in November.

What Did I Do Wrong?

In Tower of Power, we stay together because we enjoy doing what we do. We get to do something nobody else does, in that it's a very individualistic approach to playing. We're a product of our upbringing. We came up in an era where it was respected if you had your own thing. The Bay Area was a place at the time where individual effort was applauded. Having your own thing was what got you respect. All of our heroes had their own thing.

I remember in my early years with TOP, if someone came up to me and said, "Wow, that was pretty cool, you sounded like X," I was thinking, "What did I do wrong?" I never wanted to be a copy and I never wanted to remind anyone of anything other than what I was doing. All the drummers that were around here were exactly that.

Wishful Thinking

I remember when I lived in Los Angeles there was nothing close to the kind of musical community we have in the Bay Area. That's not to say there's nothing great going on there, because there certainly is. There's a level of virtuosity that I think is unmatched anywhere in the world. The players that are there are absolutely phenomenal.

While I was living there, I was approached by the leader Tim Weston, whose father was actually Paul Weston; his mother was Jo Stafford, the great singer from the 50s. His father Paul was the head of CBS records for years. Tim wanted to start a band, he approached me about it, and we put it together: Wishful Thinking. In LA there were no bands, so all the guys we got wanted to be in a band. We kept the same people together and made music for a while. We did a lot of gigs and wrote a lot of cool music.

That was a place where everyone was trying to sound like everybody else. There was no individuality; it was frowned upon. Trying to have a signature approach to your playing was frowned upon. That's because everybody was trying to get the same gigs, which were all very generic.

I lived there for 12 years, and we were the only band in town. People would come out and see us because it was a novelty. We were actually a band who used the same players without any subs.

Closet Jazz Musicians

Tower always had a master plan for the band. We never wanted to stay where we started; the thought was always evolution. We were always looking for the next step. When we decided to get a keyboard player, we found Chester Thompson, and it was the perfect thing for us, because it meant we could step up our level of performance. We had somebody who could really solo, but not in a blues way—a real soloist who had command of his instrument. He could solo over any changes, he could arrange, he could sing background vocals.

Bruce Conte grabbed me one night after rehearsal. "I want you to come check out this organ player at The Off Plaza Lounge." We went in there as CT was playing with a drummer and they're playing Top 40 soul tunes. He was playing all the melodies, all the horn parts, all the form of the song, and the range. It was very hip and very cool. He had a current playlist, and then he would play his jazz tunes. He could play everything.

I met him and we invited him to come hear our music over at Wally Heider Studios, where we were recording "What Is Hip?" We had all the tracks finished and we invited him over. It was a little surreal, because he had these really dark glasses on and a leather jacket. The glasses were so dark that he could just see out, but you couldn't see in.

We were listening to playback and he was checking us all out listening to the tunes. We asked him to be in the band. Anybody who knew about music in the Bay Area knew CT, because he was a monster player and it was an opportunity for himself.

He's a very relaxed sort of guy. His decision to come in the band was well thought out. He fit right in and became part of the family. Even today he comes to check out our shows and subs once in a while.

We were all closet jazz musicians, so we were always listening to these funky organ trios. When we brought him in, the vibe became more of an organ trio in the middle of the larger TOP.

Radar

Rocco Prestia has a real neat ability to feel music and play with a drummer. He doesn't have a lot of knowledge about what he does; he's very intuitive. He could care less what a D minor 7 chord is. He has a unique technique. It's nothing like what you are taught in school. However, he has great ears and he can fit himself into the music. He's just like radar, and when we started playing together it was an instant relationship. We never really talk much about what we're doing. We just play together and listen. I remember when I first started playing with him, I was listening to playback of some rehearsals and I noticed that when I would play on my high hat, he would play real tight short staccato notes. When I would go to my cymbal, he would play longer notes. He would match sonically what he was hearing.

One day I told him I had been listening to these tapes and I explained to him what I was hearing. I asked him, "Why do you do that?" He said, "Well, it seems like that's what I should do." It wasn't anything other than that. I thought, "Well, this is brilliant." He doesn't really have any musical training other than a real street/garage approach to playing. He's got the thing all musicians need to have, which is an intuitive sense of what to do and where to go with things. He's a complete seat-of-your-pants kind of dude. He's a joy, and we've had so many great years playing together.

PAT MARTINO

Pat Martino is one of the world's greatest guitar players and human beings. He grew up in Philly, dropped out of high school, and moved to Harlem, where he was taken in by black musicians. He played the Chitlin Circuit with Lloyd Price and at Small's Paradise in Harlem with Red Holloway and Willis Jackson. Pat made his first album as a leader in 1965 and throughout the 1970s was considered one of the most authentic and burning guitarists in the world. His style is so unique and his lines so distinct that cats such as Jerry Garcia, Pete Townshend, and Carlos Santana all sought him out and were influenced by him.

But during the 70s, Pat started having headaches that became progressively worse. Doctors thought he was depressed and psychotic. They put him in locked wards, because of the volcanic rage and anger that stemmed from the pain caused by the headaches.

By 1980 the pain had become so bad that Pat went to a neurologist, who discovered a tumor the size of a pear in his brain. He underwent emergency surgery and the tumor was successfully removed. However, when Pat came to after the surgery, he could not recognize his parents who were standing over him at his bedside. When he got home, he discovered he had lost all ability to play the guitar. The awards on the wall meant nothing, because he had no memory of them.

Seven years of intense rehabilitation went by, and with a lot of love and support Pat found his way back to the bandstand. Since that time Pat has been a shining light to musicians and music fans alike. He had found himself at the bottom of the pit and realized that was the best place to be: he had nowhere to go but up. The earnestness and sincerity of Pat exudes from his playing and how he carries himself. He has been a mentor to me, helping me focus on my true nature and breaking the bonds of my habitual nature. He has helped me focus on intention instead of results and getting out of the way of my ego.

When I started this journey to interview musicians, Pat was the first cat I reached out to. Without hesitation he agreed to come on the show. Since that day in April 2011, Pat and I have done five radio interviews. In these excerpts we talk about: being in the now, accessing reality, teaching authentically, being raised by his musical forefathers, competition, and being at the bottom of the pit.

The Bottom of the Pit

The greatest place to be is where realism is activated. That is the lowest place it can be. It is the very bottom of the pit. When you are there, you cannot go any lower than that. After that, everything is upward—that's when things really start to go upward. Until then, pursuing what is believed in—what is followed—always leads down farther, and farther, and farther to the bottom of the pit. Primarily because it has never worked—but you still believed it was going to work. It never gave what you trusted it to do—but you still believed that it would someday. It never does until you reach the bottom of the pit—and that's when it escapes and leaves you there, because it was never really interested in you to begin with. Therefore, it is at that point where faith is ignited. That's when you're lifted from within yourself. From then on, faith will always exist within you. That becomes your fuel, that becomes your belief, and that is what you follow. There's no looking back. Everything falls into place, whether you know why or you don't. But you don't care anymore, because you've been a lot lower than that for a long, long time.

I reached that point when a gentleman gave me two hours to live and a decision to make. He said, "Your brain is going to explode. I give you approximately two hours to live. You need neurosurgery immediately." Even then I still trusted in love, that I have my parents, that I'm an only child.... That I can't die out here. That I have faith I'll make it back to the East Coast.

That diagnosis took place in California. I came back to the East Coast, went to the hospital, had the neurosurgery, and that was the bottom of the pit. That was the door that opened to the bottom.

When it opened, I came out of the other side of that door, and there was nothing left: no memory, no individuals, no identity, no career, no instrumental ability, no walk of life, no purpose, none of this—a total blank blackboard. The teacher had come in and wiped the blackboard clean. Now what do you want to do? That's what you're left with. It's been up ever since.

What did give me a diagnosis—truly accurate— was technology itself. It was a computer, a CAT scan out of the hands-off mentality. It was in the hands of a machine—and the machine gave an objective realistic picture of what was wrong. Actually, nothing was wrong. It was the greatest thing that ever happened to me.

The Real Thing

The dream was to be a great musician, who was on a great album, who I had a great time trying to transcribe and copy the solo off the record player track by track, having to get another album with so many scratches on the last one by doing it so devotedly, then getting another copy— and then another and another. Well, then finally meeting some of these musicians —meeting some of these artists— in fact, being in a men's room with one of them standing next to me, and this person takes out their teeth and washes their mouth in the sink. Now, here the dream is this incredible person, who was almost made of stainless steel. A powerful artist—a superhero—took his teeth out. This is a real person. So what was I learning? I wasn't learning what I thought I was. I was learning life. I was learning what the real thing is all about.

Here's another person: I'm on a bus with these great musicians—these great artists—and I hear this argument between one artist and another artist, both famous to me. I'm still too young to realize that they're not famous—they're people! They're just like mom and pop. They're just like Uncle Joe and Uncle Paul. They're just people—and they're cursing each other; putting them down: "You don't know shit! Blah, blah, blah...." Well, what about the image I had of them as a 12-year-old? About one day wanting to meet this person? And now I have met this person, and they're saying "f*** this" and "f*** that." That ideal picture is not real — it's a distraction. But that's imagination, and that's a very healthy thing because it brings one face to face with a decision. The decision is based on interpretation and definitively comes into play into conclusion, and then a decisive change in terms of valuing.

A Study of Life itself

When I was younger, I was more interested in controlling the attention of those who were watching me, who were listening to me. As far as playing the instrument, that was always second nature. I didn't know *what* to play: that's why I was copying records at that time. I wanted attention.

The power of my artistic apparatus was my ego, which changed over the years into greater depth in terms of what my interests had become. At the beginning I wanted their attention, like an only child.

It goes far beyond the music itself. You must consider the culture that surrounds the music that amplifies the interaction. The player is only one part of the apparatus; the audience is another part of it. The surroundings that it takes place within have to be part and parcel of the history of that form of art: the sound of the room, the people who work in it, have to be pleased with the presence of it. The people who come in as customers had to come there for that reason.

You can't even touch the surface of that when you get involved in academia. The only thing that can be done is a story can be told about it, and you could absorb a general outline of the historic time.

That in some ways is distractive from what's happening right now. If I were of that age today, I would be more interested in the culture itself: social interaction within it as a vehicle for closer interaction. Gaining reward from the totality of the experience and the music is only one part of it. If that is the only thing that an individual is interested in the study of, then that person has dedicated themself to craftsmanship, not to the art. The art contains all of the other facets of the reality that surrounds these things.

Too much jazz isn't good for you. What about bluegrass music? What about classical music? What about all the other things that others enjoy? If you happen to be in a crowd of people at a certain event and it's not prone to jazz, are you supposed to be outside of this? Are you supposed to be uncomfortable in the midst of this? That's your problem, not theirs. Look how much is lost in terms of the opportunity to learn a different taste, a different food, a different culture. That's the difference between a craftsman and an artist. I think an artist is more prone to going to the essence of what art truly is, which is a much more expanded view to encase so many other different facets of living that it becomes a study of life itself.

Ignite the Intersection

Being self-taught, I have had to construct a system that works, along with what is normally prerequisite educationally for those who study music: the study of piano itself—the study of yin and yang, black and white, the keys themselves.

My study of my instrument, the guitar, has been totally different than what is taught. I have found certain things that in these clinics, master classes, seminars, symposiums I've gone out of my way to try and contribute for concern. My concern comes down to what's being revealed objectively from a third position. To see the way music has been taught—no matter what the instruments have been applied to—as opposed to seeing that prerequisite socially and culturally, and seeing a different way next to it, and not being subject to either way, but analyzing both from a central point. If you take two circles, and you push them toward each other, and then you stop them halfway in, there is a third figure—an oval. That's the place where the teacher and the student both can learn: in that central oval. That's why I'm there. I'm there to ignite the intersection. That's what I teach—not so much either side, although either side is prerequisite. They're both valuable beyond belief.

I and Me

I and me are two different identities. It's a division of oneness. ("Look what he did to me," says the encasement.) This is not "I am"—this is "me." This is our position, our expectations, our desires; our ego that eats, and makes plans to continue all these entertaining distractions, while "I" remain silent and is all that ever was, and always will be, and is energy and life in itself. These are very spiritual connotations. Once the dissected nature reveals itself to a person and they see a difference between "I am in love" versus "Wow, that feels good to me." There *is* a difference between I and me, and when that takes place, there's a decisive change in that individual's purpose: that is to get closer to what is much more ecstatic.

I was in locked wards. I was given electric shock treatment. I was given all kinds of drugs from A to Z. There were psychiatrists and psychologists, and to be honest with you, the end result was a distraction, distraction from decision itself: to be strong and concrete. I had no end conclusion as to what was taking place. All of their descriptions as to what was taking place were misdiagnosed, until finally it set itself in play due to the nature of its growth. It grew, and grew, and grew, until finally it was the size of a pear.

The next greatest distraction occurred when I said, "I'm going to take these people to court. I want to sue them. I want to get a lawyer." Wow! What a distraction that would have been. That was something I was considering amidst all sorts of turmoil inside myself: emotions that were volcanic, hatred, and anger. "How much do you want to take?" That's what this voice kept saying inside my head. "Is this what you want to go through? More and more of the same thing? So, you bring them to court—what are you going to get out of that? You're not going to make as much as the lawyers or attorneys are going to make. This is opening another doorway into a completely different arena. Is that what you're here for?"

My Enemy at the Time

I don't see the living process as a loss in any way. I see the vehicles change, but I don't see the source of the power that operates them as being subject to birth and death. I believe in life eternal; I believe in eternal life. I don't see a loss in the process; I see that a different vehicle is in process right now.

Larry Coryell was an incredible source of ideas for the music business for decades. The last time we played together was at The Blue Note in New York City. Larry had his group. It had two guitars: Larry and Vic Juris. I had my organ trio that I'm currently using. The one thing I noticed so much about Larry was as a leader, as a businessman, as an entertainer: it was incredibly serious entertainment with Larry.

In 1965 Chuck Israels was my producer. It was my first album for Vanguard Records. Vanguard Records signed me to get me off the street. Chuck brought in Ron Carter and Tommy Flanagan among others. They paid me $500 for that, which I thought was a lot of money at that time.

Primarily because they had invested a lot of money in Larry Coryell. That's how Larry and I met. Larry was my enemy at that time. He was what the record business can do to an artist if they don't know anything about how they work. Later on, when Larry and I met personally, things changed drastically. The person then came through. He wasn't really wearing the mask of the record of label.

How to Bring it About

I learned on the spot; I didn't know how to read music. I would say to Red Holloway, as they were setting up the music stands, "Red, how does this go?" I would point to where the guitar would play certain things, and Red was kind enough to quickly, softly, hum it off to me. That's how I learned, and I learned from mistakes. I learned when Slide Hampton or Onzy Matthews would point at me for a guitar solo. I would start the solo and maybe 20 bars in I would hear the rest of the band saying, "Yea, yea, yea!" That to me said a lot in regard to what I attempted to do and what I began to do. The more I attempted, the more that happened; and the more that happened, the less I gave thought to how to bring it about.

Surprise Them at the Table

The word had come out that Jerry Garcia was very interested in my playing and listened to me. It was the same way that Peter Townshend had come into my life and Carlos Santana. That particular floor of the music business became active to me when I began to visit groups like The Who. After they would do their performance at the stadium in Philadelphia, I would "pop in," where I knew they were going to have a bite to eat. The place had been cleared out, so they would have their privacy there. I knew the owners of the place. I would go in and surprise them at the table.

Schizophrenic to them

I did two albums for Warner Brothers: *Starbright* and *Joyous Lake*. When I was given the entrance into Warner, as a vehicle the first thing I did with *Starbright* was expose them to all the things that I have been interested in experiencing more of. Some of it was heavy metal, some of it was rock, some of it was blues, some of it was odd timings. When I produced that album, Warner Brothers was really stunned and shocked; they didn't know what to do with it. It was schizophrenic to them.

My producer at that particular time was Paul Rothschild. They replaced the producer that was with me when *Starbright* came out. He was producing Bonnie Raitt and a few other great artists. Paul told me why it wasn't working with *Starbright*. I said, "OK, so you want one specific thing, I guess." He replied, "Yea, that's what they want. They want one specific thing." I said, "Gimme a few weeks to put a band together and we'll do that."

I went through so many different players, auditioning them in New York City. I had two weeks left, and I had to come up with a band. In came three players out of Berklee School of Music: Delmar

Brown, electric piano and synthesizers, Mark Leonard, electric bass, and Kenwood Dennard, drums. I had written two songs in a jazz fusion kind of system. At rehearsals, when they performed, I said, "This is the band." Out came *Joyous Lake*. That kind of music became a kind of product in itself. It was very successful at that time.

Here I Am
When you begin to think positive, one of the first things to enter your mind is: "How am I supposed to stay positive when I have bills to pay, and no way to pay the fucking bills?" Well, when are the bills due? Are they due right now? Furthermore, even on the day that they're due you still have another month to pay them. For every bill, every company has to give you a margin of 30 days. All you have to do is write them a note, pick up the phone, and say, "I'm going to be a little late this month. Could I have an extension?" They'll be very happy to. At a certain point you say, "enough is enough," and that's OK. That's healthy; there's nothing wrong with it. I hear people saying to me, "Man, I don't know how you did it. That's incredible what you went through" and blah blah blah. I appreciate their respect, but it doesn't even exist anymore. The moment I came through it, I was still alive. Here I am. Why are these people looking at me? I was in my hospital bed, and my parents were staring at me, though I didn't know they were my parents. They were just another stranger looking at me. All I know is: I am, and I am here.

Realistic
After the brain operation, I had to focus much more on the moment, on now, than on what I would like it to be. No matter what it is, I'm learning something about myself in the process: my reaction, my failure to gain a positive surge of enjoyment from that moment, or the lack of it for that moment. What causes that is my desire versus reality. In the end, I hope to gain the ability to step outside and view all of these things from a neutral distance and

begin to see my identity no longer coupled with manipulation. A manipulation of music over the individual, and how he or she fits into it, how he or she is successful because of it. How he or she meets others: some are good, some are bad, because of it.

But to be at a distance and view the human experience in a much broader context. Always, in that state of mind, the only thing that's real is that the moment is now. It's difficult for me to truly participate in reality itself if I have a favorite type of reality. Reality doesn't work like that, and I have to be as realistic as possible.

The Flight Has Been Cancelled

The most important facet of staying in the moment is being solid, remaining intact.

You find yourself in a situation where you have a contractual deadline for each of the engagements, and there are legalities on those contracts as well. You find yourself in an airport, somewhere on the planet, and you know what time your flight is due to leave. Everything worked out perfectly, there you are, and suddenly that flight is delayed, and you have forty or fifty people, or maybe two hundred people, that are scheduled for that same flight. You're in line with them. You're hoping everything falls in place, and in the process your emotions are beginning to agitate. Suddenly there's an announcement that the flight has been cancelled. There's an anger that generates that is almost volcanic as an eruption within you, because it's futile and you can't fulfill what you expected to fulfill. In the process, there's anxiety that's being felt, and in the midst of that you happen to look, when it's least expected, and you see a little boy, or an elder, and they have a smile on their face. Because they're really focused on what they are doing at that point and they're not affected by this turmoil, and you wonder why you're feeling this eruption of anger within you and the painful nature of it. You envy, in a sense, that they can do that. Then in the process, you too can do that, primarily because there's nothing else you can do. It's out of your hands. You did the best you could. You should feel great about yourself, for being there, equipped and ready to go. It was taken away from you.

It's this attitude that only flourishes and grows through time. That cannot be taught. It has to be experienced, again and again and again.

See also Pat Martino with Bill Millkowski, *The Autobiography of Pat Martino* (Langham, MD: Backbeat Books 2011) and Pat Martino, *Open Road: A Documentary* (2014).

INDEX OF NAMES

Abercrombie, John 145
Abnuceals Emuukha Electric Orchestra 67
Adams, Pepper 125–26
Adams, Ryan 86, 91–92
Adderley, Cannonball 44, 136
Adepoju, Sikiru xii
Adler, Lou 29, 31
Akiyoshi, Toshiko 69
Alias, Don 45, 116
Allen, Richard "Pistol" 10, 12
Allison, Mose viii
Allman Brothers 88
Allman, Gregg 51
Asher, Peter 27, 29, 31
Ashford, Jack 10, 12
Atkins, Chet 107
Austin, Sil 57
The Australian Jazz Quintet 12
Avant, Clarence 11, 14
Axelrod, David ix
Azteca (group) 111
Babbitt, Bob 14, 38
Babbs, Ken xi–xii
Bailey, Donald 64
Baird, Mike 36
Baker, Chet 5
Baker, David N. 41, 44
Baker, Ginger 136
Balk, Harry 10, 14
Barron, Kenny 151
Basie, Count 23, 67, 120, 124
Bauer, Joe 143
The Beatles (group) 71, 75, 156
Benjamin, Benny 13
Bennett, Justine xi
Berline, Byron 35

Berry, Chuck 11
Biale, Robert xii
Birch, Gaylord 162, 164
Bishop, Elvin 51, 53
The Black Crowes (group) 91
Black Flag (group) 160
Blaine, Hal 16, 37
Blakey, Art 43
Blasucci, Sam x
Bley, Carla 134
Bley, Paul 134, 141
Blood Sweat & Tears (group) 41
Bloomfield, Mike 108
Bobo, Willie 128
Bobby and the Midnites (group) 145
Bolin, Tommy 39, 145
Boston Pops Orchestra 67–68
Boudreaux, Big Chief Monk ix
Boudreaux, Paul ix
Braunagel, Tony xii
Brecker, Michael 41, 44–46, 77, 145
Brecker, Randy 41–46, 77, 105, 118, 145
Brickman, Marshall 157
Brokensha, Jack 10, 12
Brown, Clifford 41
Brown, Dean xii
Brown, Delmar 179–80
Brown, Eddie "Bongo" 10, 12
Brown, Mel 98
Brown, Ray 44
Browne, Jackson 27, 30, 88, 153, 157
Bruce, Jack 21, 136

Budimir, Dennis 37
Bull, Sandy 157
Burbridge, Oteil xi
Burrell, Billy 126
Burrell, Kenny 98, **123–27**
Burton, Gary 108, 134–35, 141–42
Butterfield, Paul ("Butter") 51–53
Byrd, Donald 22, 124–25
Cabrera, Mr. 125
Calabro, Kevin x
Carabello, Michael 128–29
The Cardinals (group) 92
The Carpenters (group) 47, 88
Carter, Ron 8, 39, 45, 58, 116, 151–52, 178
Casal, Neal x, **81–99**
Cash, Johnny 42
Castillo, Emilio 162, 167
Castillo, Jack 167
Catherine, Philip 105, 109
Chambers, Paul 43
Chancler, Leon "Ndugu" **61–66**
Cheech and Chong 27
Cher 161
Chimenti, Jeff 96
Chinmoy, Sri 109
Chris Robinson Brotherhood (CRB) 83, 86, 91–92, 94, 99
Christian, Charlie 124
Circles Around the Sun (CATS) (group) 83, 93, 96–97
Clapton, Eric 5, 9, 16, 136
Clark, Forest 20
Clark, Guy 88
Clark, Mike 164, 166–67
Clark, Sonny 134, 139

Clinton, George 10
Cobham, Billy 35, 38–39, 41, 44, 131, **145–52**
Coffey, Dennis 10–15
Cohen, David 155
Cold Blood (group) 165, 167
Coleman, Ornette 42, 95, 119, 141
Coltrane, John (Trane) 28, 31, 44–45, 110, 118–19, 123, 138, 144
Connery, Sean 148
Conte, Bruce 169
Cooder, Ry 155
Cook, Junior 143
Coolidge, Rita xi
Corea, Chick 5, 42, 105, 111, 149
Cortez, Jerry xi
Coryell, Larry 105–10, 135, 140, 149, 178
Costner, Tom 109
Cottler, Irv 73
Country Gazette (group) 38
Cox, Sam 165
Cream (group) 135–36
Creeley, Robert 142
Crill, Chester 157
Cropper, Steve xi, 29
Crosby, David 153
Crosby, Jason 96
The Crusaders 22–26
Curtis, King 44, 57
Dauner, Wolfgang 108
Davis, Betty 132
Davis, Carlton "Santa" xii
Davis, Miles 22, 41, 43, 45, 54, 61, 64–65, 105, 109, 111, 116, 118, 121–22, 145, 147–48

Davis, Richard 58
Davis, Sammy, Jr. 19
Dawson, Alan 24
Dead Kennedys (group) 160
Delaney & Bonnie (group) 16
Densmore, John 72
DeJohnette, Jack 147
Dennard, Kenwood 180
Deodato, Eumir 132
DeShannon, Jackie 17
Desmond, Paul 23
Deutsch, Erik 96
Di Nardo, Tom 75
Diamond, Neil 47
Diggs, Butch "Horn Man" xii
Dinwiddie, Gene 53
Doerge, Craig 27
Donahue, Tom 156
Donovan 71
Dorham, Kenny 123
Dorough, Bob 134
The Doors (group) 72
Dowd, Tom 29
Dreams (group) 41
Duke, George 61, 145
Dunn, Donald "Duck" 135
Dupree, Cornell 8, 29
Duvivier, George 148
Dylan, Bob 16, 51, 53–54, 108
The Eagles (group) 55
Earle, Steve xi
El Din, Hamza 157
The Electric Flag (group) 135
Ellington, Duke 23, 106, 120, 123–24
Ellis, Don 158
Ellis, Herb 148
Ellis, Pee Wee 118
Errico, Greg 128–33, 165

Escovedo, Coke 128
Evans, Bill 110
Faier, Billy 157
Famularo, Dom xii
Farrow, Mia 71
Feinberg, Aja xii
Feinberg, Hannah xii
Feiten, Buzz 51–56
Felder, Wilton ix, 22–24
Feldhouse, Solomon 157–58
Fender, Leo 135
Ferlinghetti, Lawrence 142
Fiedler, Arthur 67–68
Findley, Chuck 74–75
Fishko, Sara 140
Flack, Roberta 57, 77
Flanagan, Tommy 124–25, 178
The Flying Machine (group) 27–28
Ford, Robben 74
Foster, Al 109
Foster, David 36
Foster, Frank 43
Foster, Gary 16
Francis, Panama 62, 137
Franklin, Aretha 29, 57, 77, 106
Free, Ronnie 139
The Free Spirits (group) 105, 108
The Flying Machine (group) 27
The Fugs (group) 28
Full Moon (group) 51
Fuller, Curtis 111
The Funk Brothers (group) 10–11, 14–15
Gadd, Steve 5–9, 76–77
Gadson, James xii, 63
Gale, Eric 78, 148

Garcia, Jerry 47–48, 128, 156, 172, 179
Garibaldi, David xi, **162–71**
Gaye, Marvin 139
Getz, Stan 134
Gibbs, Matthew Waterfall x
Gilberto, Astrud 145
Gillespie, Dizzy 41, 43, 112, 123, 133
Gillette, Mic 167
Ginty, John 86
Giuffre, Jimmy 134, 141
Gladner, Bruce 39–40
Gleeson, Dr. Patrick xii
Goffin, Gerry 27–28
Goldfinger, Dr. Tedd xii
Goldsmith, Jerry 67
Goodman, Jerry 150
Gordon, Jim 18, 37
Gordy, Berry 13–14
Gotham (group) 121
Graham Central Station (group) 165
Graham, Bill 35, 40, 136, 167–68
Graham, Larry 130
Grappelli, Stéphane 105
The Grateful Dead (group) 85, 91–92, 94–95, 97, 143, 156
Gravy, Wavy xi
Green, Grant 123–24
Gregg, Jack 143
Griffin, Paul 78
Griffith, Johnny 10, 12
Grisman, David viii
Grossman, Steve 43, 45, 118
Group Therapy (group) 37
Gruber, Brian K. 152
Gurdjieff, George 158
Guthrie, Woody 153

Guy, Buddy 134, 138
Haas, Brian x
Haden, Charlie 150
Haggard, Merle xi
Hall, Jim 8, 141, 148
Hamilton, Chico 70, 105
Hammer, Jan 39, 145, 150
Hampton, Slide 178
Hancock, Herbie 110
Handy, John 16
Hanna, Roland 8
Hard Working Americans (group) 92
Harper, Ben 153
Harper, Billy xi
Harris, Barry 125–26
Harris, Eddie 61
Harris, Sugarcane 159
Harrison, George 74–75
Hart, Mickey 128, 162
Hathaway, Donny 57
Hawes, Hampton 64
Hawkins, Coleman 22
Haynes, Roy 108, 117
Haynes, Warren 92
The Headhunters (group) 39
Helm, Levon 16, 19–20
Heminway, Jay xii
Henderson, Fletcher 106
Henderson, Joe viii, 111
Henderson, Wayne 22
Hendrix, Jimi 118, 135
Henley, Don 20, 27
Henry, Joe 86
The Heptones (group) 49
Herring, Jimmy 92, 96
Hill, Andrew 111
Hill, Jeff x
Hinkle, Rick ix

Holland, Dave 42, 118
Holland, Milt 73
Holloway, Red 172, 178
Holmes, Richard "Groove" 7
Hooker, John Lee 127
Hooper, Stix 22
Horn, Paul 70–72
Horne, Dan 94, 97
Houston, Whitney 24
Hubbard, Freddie 111, 145
Hughes, Harvey 166
Humphrey, Paul 62
Hussain, Zakir 162
Hutcherson, Bobby 16, 22
Intorre, Carmen xii
Israels, Chuck 178
Jackson, Michael 61
Jackson, Milt 145
Jackson, Paul 166–67
Jackson, Willis 172
Jagger, Mick 21
Jamal, Ahmad xi
Jamerson, James 10, 13, 35
James, Bob 5
The Jayhawks (group) 86
Jefferson Airplane (group) 143
Jim & Jessie 156
John, Dr. (Mac Rebennack) 76, 78
John, Elton 47
Jones, Booker T. 41
Jones, Elvin 43, 118, 121, 125–26
Jones, George 156
Jones, Hank 148
Jones, Philly Joe 43
Jones, Quincy 10, 14, 57, 76, 148
Jones, Rickie Lee 54
Jones, Uriel 10, 12

Jordan, Stanley 92
Joyce, James 108
Juris, Vic 178
Justo, Rodney ix
Kahn, John 47–48
Kaleidoscope (group) 153, 157–58
Kapralik, David 131
Kardashian, Kim 33
Kaye, Carol 37
Kellgren, Gary 16, 20
Keltner, Jim 16–21, 27, 33–34, 75, 155, 158
Kennedy, John F. 70
Kesey, Ken 84, 104
Kesey, Sunshine xi
Khan, Shahid Parvez xii
King, Carole 27–31
King, B. B. 76, 144
Klemmer, John 16
Knechtel, Larry 37
Knight, Ted 36
Kooper, Al 53
Kortchmar, Danny (Kooch) 20, 27–34
Kreutzmann, Bill 128
Kreutzmann, Justin 93–95
Krieger, Robby 72
Kunkel, Russell 27, 29, 31, 33
Kupka, Doc xi, 162
Kweskin, Jim 156
Kyger, Joanne 142–43
La Roca, Pete 121, 143
Laird, Rick 150
Land, Harold 61–62
Lande, Art 143
Lagos, Paul 158
Larkey, Charlie 28
Lasocki, David xiii–xiv

Lateef, Yusef 125–26
Laws, Hubert 22
Leadbelly 156
Legion of Mary (group) 47–48
Lennon, John 16, 20–21, 76
Leonard, Mark 180
Leone, Tony xi, 97
Lesh, Phil 91–92, 97
Levey, Stan 48
Levin, Tony 76
Levinger, Lowell ("Banana") 134, 142–43
Levy, Mark 94, 97
Lewis, Gary 16
Lewis, Huey xi
Lewis, Mel 48
Liebman, Dave 42, 45, **118–22**
Ligertwood, Alex xii
L'image (group) 76
Lind, Pete x
Lindley, David 16, 31, **153–61**
Little Richard 138
Lloyd, Charles 16, 34
LoCrasto, Frank x
Lodro, Sem (Jake Feinberg) x
Lookout Farm (group) 118
The Los Angeles Philharmonic 20
The Louvin Brothers 156
Ludwig, Gene 7
McCann, Les 77
McCartney, Paul 76
McClellan, Mike 156
MacDougall, Adam 92, 94, 96–98
McDuff, Jack 5, 7
McGibbon, Al 70
McKee, Sandy 162, 165

McLaughlin, John xi, 28, 54–55, 109, 145, 148–50
McLean, Don 51, 76
McLean, Jackie 111, 115
Mace, Tommy 68
Macero, Teo 109
Maharishi Mahesh Yogi v, 67, 70–72
Mahavishnu Orchestra 39, 131, 145, 150
Mainieri, Mike 76–77
Mancini, Henry 22, 67
Mangione, Chuck 5
Mangione, Gap 5
Mann, Bob xii
Mann, Herbie 105–6
Manne, Shelly 16, 48, 62, 72
Mardin, Arif 76, 78
Margen, David xii
Marian, Al 155
Marotta, Rick 33, 77
Marr, Hank 7
Marsh, George vii–viii
Martino, Pat xii, **172–82**
Masekela, Hugh 22
Mason, Harvey 60, 63
Mathis, Johnny xi
Matthews, Onzy 178
Maupin, Benny 41, 44
Mayfield, Curtis 29
Meltz, Wolfgang 35, 105
Melvoin, Mike 37
Menuhin, Yehudi 154
Menza, Don ix
Mesquite, Skip 167
Messina, Joe 10, 12
The Meters (group) 78
Metzger, Scott 96
Miller, Ethan x

Miller, Glenn 164
Miller, Steve 145
Millkowski, Bill 182
Mingus, Charles 69, 105, 154
Mitchell, Blue 22, 143
Mitchell, Joni 22
Mondavi, Michael xii
The Mongolian String Jazz Quartet (group) 152
Monk, Thelonious 61, 63–64, 139
Monnette, Ray 13
Montgomery, Monk 35
Montgomery, Wes 22, 105
Moody, James 22
Moore, Jackie 15
Moore, Mary Tyler 36
Moore, Oscar 124
Moreira, Airto xi
Morell, John ix
Mosley, Sandy 155
Mozart, Wolfgang Amadeus 108, 118
Muhoberac, Larry 49
Muñoz, Tisziji x, xii, 118
Murray, David xi
Musselwhite, Charlie 158–59
The Myddle Class (group) 28
Nash, Graham 153
Nash, Larry 60
NDR Big Band 26
Neapolitan, Ray ix
Nelson, Oliver 44, 62
New Lost City Ramblers (group) 157
Newmark, Andy 74
The Nighthawks 22
Nirvana (group) 32
Nixon, Richard 77

Nock, Mike 143
NORAD Band 164
Orbison, Roy 47
Overton, Hal 139
Ono, Yoko 76
Orbison, Roy 47
Owens, Jimmy 151
Pacific Gas and Electric (group) 39
Padorsik, Joe 13
Paley, Tom 157
Palmer, Earl 37, 62
Pang, May 20
Pantoja, Victor 128
Parisi, Jim xii
Parker, Charlie (Bird) 22–23, 43, 48, 69, 108, 136, 144, 152
Parker, Colonel Tom 49
Paul, Les 32
Pearl, Ed 155
Pedersen, Herb 38
Peña, Ralph 141
Pendarvis, Leon 149
Peraza, Armando 70, 128
Perry, Richard 21
Peterson, Oscar 23, 123
Phillips, Flip 69
Pickett, Wilson 10, 15
The Playboys (group) 16
Ponty, Jean-Luc 156
Porter, George, Jr. xi
Post, Mike 37
Powell, Bud 69
Presley, Elvis 47, 49, 138
Press, Reinie 47
Preston, Billy 74
Prestia, Rocco xi, 135, 170–71
Pretzinger, Craig xii
Price, Lloyd 172

Price, Vincent 129
Purdie, Bernard 8, 57, 78, 162
Rainey, Chuck 8, 19, **57–60**, 78
Raitt, Bonnie 179
Rakha, Alla 75
Ramsey, Willis Alan 35
Randi, Don 36
Rauch, Doug 132
The Rascals (group) 51
The Reality Sandwich (group) 167
Redbone (group) 167
Redding, Otis 139
Reeves, Martha xi
Reid, Terry 153
Reno, Don 155
Return to Forever (group) 39, 111
Rey, Alvino 159
Richards, Emil 67–75
Richard, Emilio 68
Rickert, Skip xii
Riddle, Nelson 70
Riley, Terry viii
Roach, Max 48, 62
Robinson, Chris 85, 90–91, 94, 97
Rockoff, Todd xii
Rodriguez, Sixto 10–11
The Rolling Stones (group) 8 8
Ronstadt, Linda 27
Ross, Diana 10
Rossi, Dorothy xii
Rothschild, Paul 179
Roulette, Freddie 159
Rubini, Michel 37
Rubinson, David 40, 167
Rushen, Patrice 62–63
Russell, Leon 16, 18, 35

Russo, Joe 92
Rykman, Karina xii
Sabathia, CC 109
Sabicas 155–56
Sam & Dave 106
Sample, Joe 22–26
Sandke, Randy 44
Santana (group) 129
Santana, Carlos 61, 109, 145, 172, 179
Sattui, Dario xii
Saunders, Merl 57
Sawbuck (group) 121
Scheff, Jerry 47
Scher, Farmer Dave xii
Schwartzberg, Allan xii
Scott, Ronnie 136
Scott, Shirley 5, 7
Scott, Tom 74
Scruggs, Earl 155
Seltzer, Ralph 13
Sepps, Dr. Jerry xii
Shankar, Ravi 71, 74, 154, 156
Sharrock, Sonny 106
Shaughnessy, Ed 69
Shaw, Marlena 60
Shearing, George 67, 70, 108
Shifrin, Lalo 47
Shorter, Wayne 110, 132, 149
Shrieve, Michael 129, 162
Shroeder, Carl 45
Sid Reece Big Band 163
Silver, Horace 23, 41, 43, 145–47
Simon, Carly 76–77
Simon, Paul 5, 9
Sinatra, Frank 67, 70–71
Sklar, Leland (Lee) 27, 29, 31, **35–40**, 145

Sluppik, George 97
Sly and the Family Stone (group) 128, 130, 132, 165
Smith, Jimmy 123
Smith, W. Eugene 134, 139–40
Snider, Todd 97
Snyder, Gary 143
Sousa, John Philip 164
Sparks, Willie 165
Spector, Phil 18
Spinozza, David 76–79
Stafford, Jo 169
Stanley, Ralph 156
Starks, Jabo 162
Starr, Edwin 10
Starr, Ringo 16, 18, 20
Steele, Ron ix
Steely Dan (group) 5, 55, 57, 112
Steig, Jeremy 145
Stephenson, Sam 140
Stevens, Cat 47
Stevens, Rick 162
Stewart, Bill ix
Stinson, Albert 140
Stitt, Sonny 22
Stivell, Alan 157
Stoller, Alvin 73
Stone, Chris 16, 20
Stone, Sly 128, 130–31, 133
Strayhorn, Billy 106
Streisand, Barbra viii
Stubblefield, Clyde 162
Swallow, Steve 108, **134–44**
Szabo, Gabor 16, 34, 105
Tackett, Fred ix
Tate, Grady 148
Taylor, Abbott xii
Taylor, Cecil 28, 119

Taylor, Creed 141
Taylor, Gene 143
Taylor, James 9, 27–30, 35, 40, 76–77
Tee, Richard 8, 78
The Temptations (group) 10
Ten Wheel Drive (group) 118, 121
Theodore, Mike 10–11, 13
Thielemans, Toots 151
Thigpen, Ed 69
Thompson, Chester 169–70
Tjader, Cal 128
Titelman, Russ 9
Tolstoy, Leo 108
Tower of Power (group) xi, 162–63, 165, 167–68
Townshend, Pete 172, 179
Tristano, Lennie 120
Truchard, Anthony xii
Trucks, Butch xi
Tutt, Ron 47–50
Tyrell, Steve 38
Uncle Tupelo (group) 86
Van Dyke, Earl 10, 12
Van Zandt, Townes 88
Vaughan, Sarah 45, 150
Vinnegar, Leroy 64
The Virginia Boys (group) 156
Vitous, Miroslav 132, 149
Vitt, Bill 165
Waldman, Gary 90
Walker, David T. 29, 60
Walker, George xii
Walker, Junior 44
Walker, T-Bone 134, 138
Waller, Fats 23
War (group) 39
Washington, Grover, Jr. 145

Watanabe, Sadeo 69
Weather Report (group) 61, 132
Weeks, Willie 74
Wein, George 138
Weinberg, Max xi
Weir, Bob xi
West, Bobby 37
Weston, Paul 169
Weston, Tim 169
Wexler, Jerry 10, 15
White, Lenny 105, **111–17**
White, Robert 10, 12
Whitfield, Norman 14
The Who (group) 179
Williams, Andy 37
Williams, John 67, 72
Williams, John B. 41
Williams, Lenny 162
Williams, Mason 37, 104
Williams, Tony 45, 112, 116
Willis, Eddie 10, 12–13
Willis, Larry 151
Wilson, Gerald 62
Wishful Thinking (group) 169
Wolfgang (group) 39–40
Wonder, Stevie 51, 167
The Wrecking Crew (group) 29, 36–37
YES (group) 91
Yong, Kim xi
Young, Lester 120, 136
The Youngbloods (group) 143
Zappa, Frank 67
Zawinul, Joe 128, 132–33, 149
Zeitlin, Denny viii
Zephyr (group) 39
Zevon, Warren 27, 153
Zigmund, Eliot 143
Zuckerberg, Mark xi

Made in the USA
Monee, IL
16 July 2020